D0646829

cooking
Italian
with kids

Liz Franklin
photography by Lisa Linder

cooking
Italian
with kids

RYLAND
PETERS
& SMALL
LONDON NEW YORK

Senior designer Megan Smith
Senior editor Céline Hughes
Location & model research
   Emily Westlake
Production manager
   Patricia Harrington
Art director Leslie Harrington
Publishing director Alison Starling

Food stylist Joy Skipper
Prop stylist Liz Belton
Indexer Sandra Shotter

First published in the
United States in 2008 by
Ryland Peters & Small, Inc.
519 Broadway, 5th Floor
New York, Ny 10012

www.rylandpeters.com

10 9 8 7 6 5 4 3 2 1

Text © Liz Franklin 2008
Design and photographs
© Ryland Peters & Small 2008

ISBN: 978-1-84597-698-9

All rights reserved. No part of this
publication may be reproduced,
stored in a retrieval system, or
transmitted in any form or by any
means, electronic, mechanical,
photocopying, or otherwise,
without the prior permission
of the publisher.

A CIP record for this book is available
from the Library of Congress.

Printed and bound in China

• All fruit and vegetables should
be thoroughly washed before eating
or cooking.

• All spoon measurements are level,
unless otherwise specified.

• Ovens should be preheated to the
specified temperature. Recipes in
this book were tested using a regular
oven. If using a convection oven,
follow the manufacturer's instructions
for adjusting temperatures.

• All eggs are medium, unless
otherwise specified. Recipes
containing raw or partially cooked
egg, or raw fish or shellfish, should
not be served to the very young, very
old, anyone with a compromised
immune system, or pregnant women.

contents

buon appetito!

"A tavola!" is a familiar and happy cry in houses all over Italy at mealtimes: it's the call for everyone to drop what they're doing and come to the table to eat, whether for a simple lunch or a sumptuous feast.

From the humblest means all the way up to aristocracy, Italians have a very special attitude to food; eating is not about simply refuelling or self-indulgence, but about sitting down together around the table and enjoying the companionship of others. Mealtimes are a time for family and friends to meet en masse, to enjoy lovely food, chat, and delight in each other's company, listen to each other's news, and reflect on one another's day.

Despite the hustle and bustle of the rush-around lives we seem to live now, when it comes to food, the Italians still seem to have their priorities firmly set. Generally speaking, neither the preparation of food nor the eating of it is a hurried affair—although naturally in the 21st century there are always exceptions! This means that, for the most part, Italian children grow up from an early age with a love of good food; they also develop discerning palates, get to know about ingredients, learn about table manners, and, often as an added bonus, discover the art of conversation too! All of these are important factors to those of us concerned about the damage that junk food and eating on the run are doing to our health and social skills.

In Italy particularly, cooking is rarely considered a chore, but rather an act of love. Passing down beloved kitchen secrets and recipes through generations is something that still goes on, and doing so is all part of the native passion for good food. Mamma's and Nonna's (Grandma's) recipes are usually considered the best by their loyal descendants and looked upon as precious treasure!

For children, helping in the kitchen is always an exciting thing to do—all those fabulous ingredients to chop and stir; the enticing smells; the textures and colors; the little nibbles and tastes along the way. And at the end of it, the very special feeling when they proudly show off their efforts to family and friends and see the delight as everyone tucks into the fruits of their labors. Imagine then how full of pride the youngsters in your life will be if the recipes are actually aimed at them and you are merely the one helping out with the tricky bits and the hot spots (plus the shopping before and the washing-up after!)

This book is packed with delicious Italian recipes that I have shared with my own three sons, Chris, Oliver, and Tim. All four of us have always had a great passion for Italian food, and now we are lucky enough to have a house there, every day seems to bring new and delicious discoveries.

Some of the recipes that follow are based on dishes we've eaten in restaurants or cafés, or bought in pastry stores or even supermarkets. Some are influenced by classics, while others are borrowed from our Italian friends and tweaked the tiniest bit to take into account the difference in available ingredients outside Italy. I've tried to offer simple, child-friendly family recipes rather than those that will appeal only to young appetites, thereby encouraging the whole extended family to join in and appreciate the pleasure that home-cooked food can bring.

In a truly Italian way, some of the recipes in this book are full of goodness and the freshest ingredients, and others are meant to be occasional treats for those with a sweet tooth. I hope you enjoy sharing them with your children, and who knows, maybe they will carry some of them along through life and in time pass them on to their children too.

italian essentials

EXTRA VIRGIN OLIVE OIL (OLIO EXTRA VERGINE DI OLIVA)

There are lots of kinds of olive oil, but the best and healthiest is extra virgin olive oil. I always use this type in all my cooking—sometimes I even make cakes with it! You don't have to use an expensive one for cooking; a supermarket own brand should be good enough as long as it is labeled extra virgin. You could pay a little more for a special one to drizzle on salads though. Always use extra virgin in the recipes in this book.

BASIL (BASILICO)

Basil has such a sunny, cheery smell; it always reminds me of Italy, perhaps because it goes so well in delicious tomato sauces and salads, on pizza, and with pasta. Make sure you use only the freshest basil with perky green leaves —no black, droopy bits! You can easily grow it in pots on a sunny windowsill in the summer. For the best results, always add it to dishes at the last minute, and don't chop it, as you will lose some of the flavor. Tear it instead—it's less fussy that way anyway.

BAY LEAVES (ALLORO)

Bay leaves find their way into a lot of dishes in Italian cooking. They add a lovely subtle flavor to pasta sauces, soups, and casseroles, and I add them to rice pudding too. Fresh bay leaves are good, but you can dry the leaves whole and simply pop them in a screw-top jar.

OREGANO (ORIGANO)

Fresh oregano isn't always easy to find, but it dries well, so it's a good idea to keep a jar in the cupboard for tomato-based sauces and to scatter over pizza when you can't get hold of fresh basil. If you're buying it in the supermarket's dried herbs and spices section, try to find the freeze-dried kind, which has a much better flavor.

PARSLEY (PREZZEMOLO)

Italian parsley is the flatleaf kind rather than the very frilly kind usually known as curly parsley. Parsley is probably used in Italian cooking even more than basil is—in all kinds of soups, stews, and sauces. You can grow it in a pot on a windowsill; you can even freeze fresh parsley and crumble it straight from the freezer into sauces and such as you need it.

ROSEMARY (ROSMARINO)

Rosemary is another herb that is used a lot in Italian cooking; it's used to flavor roast meats and vegetables. It makes a fantastic flavoring for focaccia too—see the recipe on page 30. Always try to use fresh rosemary, as dried isn't really very nice at all.

SAGE (SALVIA)

Sage is another well-loved herb in Italian dishes and it's especially lovely with pork. It's also ultra delicious with pumpkin belly button pasta parcels, as I hope you will agree when you try the recipe on page 26!

PARMESAN CHEESE (PARMIGIANO REGGIANO)

Real Italian Parmesan cheese is a very special cheese indeed; it is also called Parmigiano Reggiano and carries a special official certificate to prove that it has passed very strict standards and been produced only in certain areas. It is known as the King of Italian Cheeses and is fabulous grated over soups and pasta, shaved onto salads, or stirred into risottos—but do buy a whole piece and grate it as you need it because ready-grated Parmesan just doesn't have the same flavor.

PANCETTA (PANCETTA)

Pancetta is a type of Italian bacon; it comes whole or in matchstick pieces called lardons. You can buy it easily in Italian specialty shops. It is used in sauces and casseroles.

GARLIC (AGLIO)

Garlic isn't a particularly Italian ingredient but many of the recipes in Italian cuisine wouldn't be the same without it. Don't worry, Italian dishes don't often taste very strongly of garlic —it's used to help add a subtle flavor. Be careful not to fry it at high temperatures, as it turns bitter and yucky if it gets too brown.

TOMATOES (POMODORI)

It's difficult to imagine Italian food without thinking about tomatoes. In Italy there are some wonderful varieties and they come in all shapes and sizes—it's often the funny-looking ones that taste the best! At home, choose plump, juicy ripe tomatoes in the summer, but in the winter months it can often be best to use good-quality canned tomatoes. I love using the little cherry ones you can buy in cans now—they have a lovely sweet flavor and make the most delicious sauce.

SETTING A PRETTY TABLE

There's nothing especially Italian about setting a pretty table at which to eat, but it makes everyone feel good if they are in pleasant surroundings. You may like to lay a tablecloth, place mats, and serviettes—mats will protect the table and serviettes always come in handy for wiping mouths and hands when you've been slurping spaghetti or tucking into a big slice of pizza! For special meals, you might like to add a few flowers. You don't need to go to the trouble of using a fancy vase—a simple drinking glass can look just as good.

KITCHEN EQUIPMENT

You are likely to have most of the kitchen equipment needed to prepare and cook all the recipes in your kitchen at home already; weighing scales, mixing bowls, wooden spoons, cutting boards, knives, whisks, a rolling pin, cookie cutters (although you can use an upside-down glass), saucepans, cake pans, baking sheets etc. If you wanted to treat yourself to a pasta maker or an ice-cream maker, they are great tools for any budding Italian chef to have and they aren't too expensive. Of course, you can make the pasta and ice cream without them, but they do make life a little easier if you love pasta and ice cream as much as we do in our house.

People seem to love pasta the world over, but as you would expect, none so much as the Italians. The Italians eat pasta every day—and I do mean every day. I used to be amazed when I looked inside other people's carts at my local supermarket in Italy; most of them seemed to include not two or three packets of pasta, as you might imagine, but probably nearer a dozen and sometimes more! Ninety percent of Italians eat dried pasta, the most popular brand being De Cecco, and every cart I saw seemed to have a little mountain of the familiar blue and yellow packages. There was an assortment of spaghetti, linguine, penne, farfalle, fusilli, cavatappi—swirls, curls, strands, tubes, and bows. Different shapes for different sauces: chunky shapes and wide ribbons for rich, meaty sauces; fine lengths and thin strands for delicate sauces.

Pasta is quick to cook and healthy too (as long as you don't eat your way through mountains of it and sit around on your bottom afterwards!) Marathon runners eat lots of pasta. During the children's cookery classes I used to run, the children loved to make fresh pasta. I used to giggle and chant at the start of the class "pasta, pasta, makes you go faster."

pasta

This is possibly the most important—and simplest—Italian recipe you'll ever need. Master this and there will be a world of scrumptious meals at your fingertips!

basic egg pasta

2¼ cups Italian "oo" type
  flour, plus extra to
  sprinkle
a pinch of salt
3 eggs
a pasta machine (optional)

Serves 4

1 Sift the flour and salt into a large bowl. Make a well in the center and add the eggs. If you like, you can use a food processor instead—just **ask an adult to help you** put the flour, salt, and eggs in the bowl of the food processor ready for mixing.

2 Bring the mixture together by mixing the ingredients with your fingertips, or press the "pulse" button on the food processor repeatedly to make the ingredients combine. You should have a soft but not sticky dough.

3 Sprinkle a little flour on a clean work surface, turn the dough out onto it, and knead (see Tip on the next page) for 4–5 minutes. Wrap the dough in plastic wrap and put in the fridge for at least 30 minutes before using.

4 If you have a pasta machine, set the lasagne rollers to the widest setting. Take a quarter of the pasta dough out of the fridge and keep the remaining dough wrapped in plastic wrap.

5 Flatten your small lump of dough until it fits through the rollers of the machine. **Ask an adult to help you** flatten the dough by passing it through the machine.

6 Take the flattened dough and fold it into 3. Run it through the machine again and then fold it into 3 once more. Repeat this process another 3 times, so that the dough has gone through the machine on the same setting a total of 5 times. The dough should be nice and smooth and pliable.

7 Reduce the roller width by one notch and pass the pasta through again.

8 Repeat the process, reducing the roller width by one notch each time. You may have to cut the pasta sheet in half to fit into the machine. If you do, remember to keep the dough you are not working with covered with plastic wrap because it will become too dry to work with if it is left exposed to the air for too long.

9 Once the dough has been through the smallest roller width, you can then make spaghetti, tagliatelle, or pappardelle by passing your sheet of pasta through the right settings of your machine (follow the instructions in the manual), or you can ask an adult to help you cut the pasta sheets with a knife. Alternatively, you can use the sheets to make lasagne, ravioli (page 24), or belly button pasta parcels (page 26).

10 If you don't have a pasta machine, you will need to sprinkle a little flour on a clean work surface and roll out the dough with a rolling pin. It will take some effort and strength to get the dough super-thin, but keep at it! It may be easier for you to roll out a quarter of the dough at a time (remember to keep the remaining dough wrapped in plastic wrap so that it doesn't dry out).

TIP To knead dough, push the heels of your hands into the lump of dough and squash down. Swivel the dough around slightly and squash down again. Keep swivelling and turning the dough over so that you are kneading it evenly all over. If it gets too flat, fold the dough over onto itself to make it into a lump again and keep kneading. It's hard work, but it's worth it—when you've finished you'll have a firm, smooth, gorgeously stretchy dough!

This is a lovely easy sauce that bubbles away to become deliciously sticky. It's a little like spaghetti Bolognese.

tagliatelle with rich meat sauce
tagliatelle con sugo di carne

1 recipe tagliatelle (page 12)
  or 14 oz storebought
  dried tagliatelle
salt and black pepper
freshly grated Parmesan,
  to serve

For the sauce
1 onion
1 carrot
2 garlic cloves
1 celery rib
3 tablespoons olive oil
1 lb ground beef
14-oz can cherry tomatoes
  (or regular chopped)
1¼ cups beef broth
1 teaspoon sugar
1 teaspoon mixed dried
  herbs

Serves 4

1 To make the sauce, **ask an adult to help you** peel the onion and carrot and chop them finely. Peel the garlic cloves (see Tip on page 18) and crush them with a garlic crusher. Trim the ends of the celery and pull off some of the nasty stringy bits from the outside. Chop the celery finely.

2 **Ask an adult to help you** heat the olive oil in a saucepan and fry the onion, carrot, garlic, and celery over gentle heat for 5–6 minutes, until everything is soft but not colored.

3 Add the ground beef to the saucepan and break it up into pieces with a wooden spoon. Leave it to cook for 5 minutes, stirring occasionally, until it has turned brown all over.

4 Stir in the canned tomatoes, broth, sugar, and mixed herbs, then season with a little salt and black pepper. Let the sauce bubble for about 25 minutes, until it has reduced and is glossy and thick.

5 In the meantime, **ask an adult to help you** cook the tagliatelle. Bring a big saucepan of water to a boil and add a pinch of salt. Drop in the tagliatelle and cook for about 2 minutes if you've made it fresh, or according to the instructions on the package if you bought it dried, from a store. The tagliatelle is ready when it is "al dente" (see Tip below).

6 Drain the pasta and toss with the sauce. Serve at once with freshly grated Parmesan.

TIP To check if pasta is perfectly cooked, **ask an adult to help you** fish out a strand of tagliatelle (or whatever type of pasta you are cooking) from the hot water, blow on it till it's cool enough to eat, then carefully take a bite. The pasta should be soft but not soggy, and should still retain a little bite to it. When it's cooked like this, it's called al dente!

Adding eggs to the sauce in this recipe gives it a lovely buttery taste and texture. Pappardelle are big, wide ribbons of pasta—great for rich, tasty sauces like this one.

pappardelle with pancetta, eggs & tomato
pappardelle con pancetta, uova e pomodori

1 recipe pappardelle
    (page 12) or 14 oz
    storebought dried
    pappardelle
3 egg yolks
salt and black pepper
freshly grated Parmesan,
    to serve (optional)

For the sauce
1 onion
2 garlic gloves
3 tablespoons olive oil
5 oz pancetta, cut into
    matchsticks
14-oz can cherry tomatoes
    (or regular chopped)
2 teaspoons sugar
a small handful of fresh
    basil leaves, torn

Serves 4

1 To make the sauce, **ask an adult to help you** peel the onion and chop it finely. Peel the garlic cloves (see Tip on page 18) and crush them with a garlic crusher.

2 **Ask an adult to help you** heat the olive oil in a saucepan and fry the pancetta, onion, and garlic for 5–6 minutes over gentle heat until everything is soft but not colored.

3 Stir in the canned tomatoes and sugar, then season with a little salt and black pepper. Let the sauce bubble for about 20 minutes, until it has reduced and is glossy and thick.

4 Add the basil and let the sauce simmer gently for 5 minutes more.

5 In the meantime, **ask an adult to help you** cook the pappardelle. Bring a big saucepan of water to a boil and add a pinch of salt.

Drop in the pappardelle and cook it for about 2 minutes if you've made it fresh, or according to the instructions on the package if you bought it dried, from a store. The pappardelle is ready when it is "al dente" (see Tip on page 14).

6 Put the egg yolks in a bowl and beat with a fork until smooth.

7 Drain the cooked pasta and toss with the sauce. Remove from the heat and immediately add the egg yolks, tossing the pasta quickly so that the heat of the sauce cooks the eggs without being so hot that they scramble and get lumpy.

8 Serve at once with freshly grated Parmesan, if you like.

This is the simplest of pasta dishes; but the simplest food can often be the most magical. If you like hot peppers, there is a similar dish to this that includes a couple of chopped chiles or a pinch of dried pepper flakes with the garlic-infused olive oil. Never be afraid to experiment—that's how we discover new things!

spaghetti with herbs & garlic
spaghetti alle erbe e aglio

1 recipe spaghetti (page 12)
  or 14 oz storebought
  dried spaghetti
a pinch of salt
1 unwaxed lemon
a large handful of mixed
  fresh herbs (such as
  chives, parsley, and
  basil), leaves torn
½ cup olive oil
3 garlic cloves
freshly grated Parmesan,
  to serve

Serves 4

1 **Ask an adult to help you** cook the spaghetti. Bring a big saucepan of water to a boil and add the salt. Drop in the spaghetti and cook it for about 2 minutes if you've made it fresh, or according to the instructions on the package if you bought it dried, from a store. The spaghetti is ready when it is "al dente" (see Tip on page 14).

2 Wash the lemon and **ask an adult to help you** grate the zest (see Tip on page 24).

3 While the spaghetti is cooking, **ask an adult to help you** heat the oil in a skillet over medium heat.

4 Peel the garlic cloves (see Tip below). Add the whole cloves to the skillet and let warm and infuse the oil for 3–4 minutes.

5 **Ask an adult to help you** fish the garlic out of the oil with a slotted spoon.

6 Drain the pasta and toss with the infused oil, the lemon zest, and the herbs. Serve at once with freshly grated Parmesan.

TIP It can be tough to peel a garlic clove as the skin tends to stick to the garlic. Here's an easy trick: put the clove flat on a cutting board. Take a wide, blunt knife and place it, flat-side down, on top of the clove and push down hard with your hand. This loosens the skin and makes peeling much quicker!

This is a favorite in our house. It's good if you have to cook for someone who doesn't eat meat, but it's such a delicious mixture of flavors and textures that everyone seems to love it. Farfalle is Italian for "butterflies," which is exactly what these pasta shapes look like. I think they're perfect for this recipe—although any short pasta shape would work nicely, so if you have a particular favorite, don't be afraid to try it!

pasta butterflies with zucchini, golden raisins & pine nuts
farfalle con zucchine, sultanine e pinoli

2 tablespoons golden raisins
3 medium zucchini
2 garlic cloves
3 tablespoons olive oil
3 tablespoons pine nuts
1 unwaxed lemon
14 oz dried farfalle
salt and black pepper
Poor Man's Parmesan (page 85), to serve (optional)

Serves 4

1 Put the raisins into a little dish and cover them with hot water. Leave them for about 15 minutes, until they are nice and plump.

2 **Ask an adult to help you** trim the zucchini and cut them into thin slices.

3 Peel the garlic cloves (see Tip on page 18) and crush them with a garlic crusher.

4 **Ask an adult to help you** heat the olive oil in a large saucepan, then fry the zucchini over medium heat for 6–8 minutes, until they are golden; you will need to give them a good stir now and again.

5 Add the pine nuts and cook for a further 2–3 minutes, until the pine nuts are golden.

6 Add the garlic and cook for just 2 minutes; you don't want it to cook so much that it browns, which is when it becomes bitter.

7 Wash the lemon and ask an adult to help you grate the zest (see Tip on page 24).

8 Drain the raisins and stir them into the mixture together with the lemon zest. Season the mixture to taste with some salt and black pepper.

9 In the meantime, **ask an adult to help you** cook the pasta. Bring a big saucepan of water to a boil and add a pinch of salt. Drop in the pasta and cook according to the instructions on the package. The cooked pasta should be "al dente" (see Tip on page 14).

10 Drain the pasta and toss with the zucchini mixture. Serve at once with Poor Man's Parmesan scattered over, if you like.

The first time I ate this dish with my three sons was on an old-fashioned sailing ship in the crystal-clear waters of northern Sardinia. It is such a simple dish; the skipper could prepare it for us even with the very basic galley and single cooking element that was on the boat, but it tasted wonderful. We still eat it at home all the time, and it always makes us feel sunny inside, whatever the weather!

penne with tomatoes, garlic & basil
penne con pomodori, aglio e basilico

14 oz ripe cherry tomatoes
2 garlic cloves
½ cup olive oil
**a small handful of fresh
  basil leaves, torn**
14 oz dried penne
salt and black pepper

Serves 4

1 **Ask an adult to help you** chop the cherry tomatoes in half.

2 Peel the garlic cloves (see Tip on page 18) and crush them with a garlic crusher.

3 Pop the tomatoes and garlic into a large bowl. Pour over the olive oil. Season with salt and black pepper, add half the basil, and leave for an hour or so to infuse. A warm place is best, or at room temperature, but not the fridge because the cold will stop the oil from absorbing all the lovely flavors.

4 **Ask an adult to help you** cook the pasta. Bring a big saucepan of water to a boil and add a pinch of salt. Drop in the pasta and cook according to the instructions on the package. The cooked pasta should be "al dente" (see Tip on page 14).

5 Drain the pasta and add it to the bowl with the infused oil. Toss well so that the oil coats all the pieces and finally stir in the remaining torn basil.

This is an easy-peasy one-dish supper for the whole family—just as yummy as a lasagne but much less work!

big pasta shells stuffed with herbs & ricotta
conchiglioni farciti con erbe e ricotta

14 oz dried big pasta shells
a pinch of salt
3 tomatoes
16 oz ricotta cheese
2 tablespoons mixed fresh herbs (such as chives, parsley, and basil)
3 tablespoons olive oil
3 tablespoons freshly grated Parmesan
a crisp, green salad, to serve
an ovenproof serving dish

Serves 4

1 **Ask an adult to help you** preheat the oven to 350°F.

2 **Ask an adult to help you** cook the pasta. Bring a big saucepan of water to a boil and add the salt. Drop in the pasta and cook according to the instructions on the package. The cooked shells should be "al dente" (see Tip on page 14). Drain and set aside.

3 In the meantime, **ask an adult to help you** chop the tomatoes in half. Scoop out the seeds and center with a spoon. Chop the tomatoes into small pieces and transfer them to a bowl.

4 Stir in the ricotta and mixed herbs.

5 Place a teaspoonful of the mixture into each of the pasta shells and lay them snugly in your ovenproof serving dish.

6 Drizzle over the olive oil and scatter over the Parmesan. **Ask an adult to help you** transfer the dish to the preheated oven and bake for 10 minutes, until hot. Serve with a nice crisp, green salad.

Big floppy parcels of tuna and cheese make a lovely supper. They are much easier to make than you might think and yet they look very impressive!

tuna ravioli

ravioli al tonno

1 recipe Basic Egg Pasta
 (page 12, Steps 1–3 only)
a pinch of salt

For the filling
2 slices of white bread
two 8-oz cans tuna in olive
 oil, drained
½ cup freshly grated
 Parmesan
⅓ cup ricotta cheese

To serve
3 tablespoons butter
a small bunch of fresh
 chives, snipped into pieces
 with kitchen scissors
1 small unwaxed lemon
 (optional)
a pastry wheel (optional)
parchment paper, dusted
 with semolina

Serves 4

1 To make the filling, **ask an adult to help you** cut the crusts off the bread and whiz the bread in a food processor until you get crumbs.

2 Put the bread crumbs, tuna, Parmesan, and ricotta together in a large bowl and mix with a fork until well combined and quite smooth. Set aside.

3 Follow Steps 4–10 on page 12.

4 Cut the piece of pasta into 2 pieces roughly the same shape and size.

5 Sprinkle a little flour over a clean work surface and lay the 2 pieces of pasta out onto it. Cover one piece with plastic wrap.

6 Place teaspoonfuls of the tuna filling at even intervals in a row across one half of the pasta. Fold the edge nearest you over to meet the edge that is furthest away and let it fall loosely over the filling. Press firmly around the filling to seal the pasta, then cut into squares using a sharp knife or pastry wheel. Lay the ravioli out on the prepared parchment paper.

7 Repeat with the rest of the pasta dough.

8 Ask an adult to help you cook the ravioli. Bring a big saucepan of water to a boil and add the salt. Drop in the ravioli and cook for 2–3 minutes until they rise to the surface and are "al dente" (see Tip on page 14).

9 In the meantime, **ask an adult to help you** melt the butter in a large skillet over medium heat. Add the chives. Drain the pasta and toss it into the butter, stirring gently. Cook for 2–3 minutes, until the pasta is well coated in the butter and is nice and hot.

10 If you'd like some lemon zest in your pasta too, wash the lemon and **ask an adult to help you** grate the zest (see Tip below). Sprinkle the lemon zest over your ravioli and serve.

TIP To grate a lemon or any citrus fruits, take a citrus zester and **ask an adult to help you** grate the zest. Avoid grating any of the white pith (underneath the colored skin of the fruit), as this is bitter.

belly button pasta parcels stuffed with pumpkin
tortellini farciti con zucca

1 recipe Basic Egg Pasta
  (page 12, Steps 1–3 only)
3 tablespoons butter
8 fresh sage leaves
salt and black pepper

For the filling
8 oz pumpkin or butternut
  squash
leaves from 3–4 sprigs
  of fresh thyme
2 tablespoons olive oil
4 tablespoons ricotta
  cheese
1/2 cup freshly grated
  Parmesan, plus extra
  to serve
a pastry wheel
parchment paper, dusted
  with semolina

Serves 4

1 **Ask an adult to help you** preheat the oven to 400°F.

2 Ask an adult to help you peel the pumpkin or squash, remove the seeds, and cut the flesh into small chunks. Put in a roasting pan and scatter over the thyme.

3 Drizzle with olive oil, season with salt and black pepper, and toss well using your hands. **Ask an adult to help you** put the roasting pan in the preheated oven and roast for 25 minutes, until soft and golden.

4 **Ask an adult to help you** remove the roasting pan from the oven, then let cool. When cool, transfer to a bowl and mash with a fork until smooth. You can use a food processor or stick blender if you prefer.

5 Stir in the ricotta and Parmesan, have a little taste and if you think it needs a touch more salt or pepper, then add some.

6 Follow Steps 4–10 on page 12.

7 Cut the piece of pasta into 2 pieces roughly the same shape and size.

8 Sprinkle a little flour over a clean work surface and lay the 2 pieces of pasta out onto it. Cover one piece with plastic wrap.

9 Place teaspoonfuls of the filling at even intervals in a row across one half of the pasta. Leave a space of about 1 inch between each little pile.

10 Fold the edge nearest to you over to meet the edge that is furthest away and let it fall loosely over all the little mountains of filling. Using a finger, push the pasta dough gently but firmly around the pasta dough, to seal in the filling. Make sure you have no big bubbles of air. It might take a little practice, but it's fun and very satisfying when you can do it!

11 Use a pastry wheel to cut little semi-circles, leaving a 1/4-inch border around the filling. Press around the edges again to make sure the packages are tightly sealed.

12 Take hold of one of the filled shapes at each corner, pull them together until they meet, and pinch them together tightly. You should end up with a plump belly button.

These little pumpkin pasta parcels look just like belly buttons and come from the town of Bologna. They're lots of fun to make and taste absolutely yummy!

13 Repeat with all the filled parcels, then lay them on the prepared parchment paper.

14 Repeat the whole process with the rest of the pasta.

15 Ask an adult to help you cook the tortellini. Bring a big saucepan of water to a boil and add a pinch of salt. Drop in the tortellini and cook for 2–3 minutes, until the tortellini parcels rise to the surface and are "al dente" (see Tip on page 14).

16 In the meantime, **ask an adult to help you** melt the butter in a large skillet over medium heat. Add the sage so that the butter becomes infused while it melts. Drain the pasta and toss it into the butter, stirring gently. Cook for 2–3 minutes, until the pasta is well coated in the butter and is nice and hot. Serve at once, with extra Parmesan.

Bread is the foundation of the Italian diet; so much so that Italians generally buy fresh bread every day and it is the first thing to go on the lunch or dinner table. Even the smallest villages still have bakeries and there you can usually find a selection of breads which varies throughout Italy from region to region.

Having such lovely bakeries means that it is unusual for people to bake at home. However, many of us outside Italy aren't so lucky and local bakeries are a rare thing. Fortunately, baking bread at home can be great fun and satisfying.

Another Italian staple is polenta—a kind of cornmeal that has become very trendy outside Italy but was traditionally a food of the poor. When meat and fresh food were scarce during the Second World War, it was a staple of the Italian diet. Polenta was eaten with a little cheese or wild mushrooms to fill you up.

Plain polenta has little taste and a texture like rough semolina, but teamed with cheese or cooked as a dessert, it's scrumptious. Traditionally, it was very slow to prepare but these days there are instant brands readily available in supermarkets. Some Italians would throw their hands up in horror at the idea of using them, whilst others welcome the shortcut. I would encourage you to use them!

bread & polenta

This heavenly bread is so delicious and satisfying—and easy too!

rosemary focaccia
focaccia con rosmarino

6 tablespoons olive oil

a large bunch of fresh
   rosemary, leaves only

3¾ cups bread flour, plus
   extra to sprinkle

1 envelope (7 g) fast-acting
   dry yeast

1 teaspoon salt

about ¾ cup warm water
   (see Tip below right)

coarse salt

*a baking sheet, about
   8 x 12 inches, dusted
   with flour*

Makes one loaf

1 Put the olive oil and rosemary into a bowl. Squeeze the rosemary with your hands to infuse the oil.

2 Put the flour, yeast, and salt into a bowl and stir well. Stir in 2 tablespoons of the rosemary-infused olive oil and 1–2 tablespoons warm water. Put your hands right in the bowl and mix the ingredients with your fingers. Keep adding warm water, a little at a time, until you get a soft but not sticky dough.

3 Sprinkle a little flour over a clean work surface, turn the dough out onto it, and knead for 5–10 minutes (see Tip on page 13). The dough should be very smooth and pliable.

4 Using a rolling pin, roll the dough out into a rectangle slightly smaller than the prepared baking sheet. Lift it carefully into the sheet, cover the sheet with a clean kitchen towel, and let rise in a warm place for about 1 hour, until the dough is double the original size.

5 **Ask an adult to help you** preheat the oven to 400°F.

6 Uncover the dough, which should be almost bursting out of the baking sheet by now! Push your thumb all over it (don't worry if this deflates it) to make big dimples. Scatter some coarse salt over the top.

7 **Ask an adult to help you** put the bread in the preheated oven and bake for about 20–25 minutes. **Ask an adult to help you** test the bread—it should be firm and golden and sound hollow when tapped on its bottom!

8 Let cool on a wire rack and serve cut into squares.

TIP The warm water used to make bread dough should be about as warm as your hands. So if you put your fingers in a bowl of the water, it should feel nice and warm—neither too hot nor too cold.

These mini-focaccias taste fantastic all on their own, although you could fill them to make sandwiches too. They make great picnic or lunchbox food.

mini-focaccias with zucchini
focaccine alle zucchine

3 cups bread flour
1 envelope (7 g) fast-acting dry yeast
3 tablespoons olive oil
about 3/4 cup warm water (see Tip on page 30)
2 small zucchini
salt
2 large baking sheets, dusted with flour

Makes 8

1 Put the flour, yeast, and 1 teaspoon salt into a bowl and stir well. Stir in just 2 tablespoons of the olive oil and 1–2 tablespoons warm water. Put your hands right in the bowl and mix the ingredients with your fingers. Keep adding warm water, a little at a time, until you get a soft but not sticky dough.

2 Sprinkle a little flour over a clean work surface, turn the dough out onto it, and knead for 5–10 minutes (see Tip on page 13). The dough should be very smooth and pliable.

3 Divide the dough into 8 pieces and knead each piece again until smooth. Using a rolling pin, roll each piece into small circles just over 1/2 inch thick. Lay the circles, spaced well apart, on the prepared baking sheets and let rise in a warm place for about 40 minutes, until double their original size.

4 **Ask an adult to help you** preheat the oven to 425°F.

5 **Ask an adult to help you** trim the zucchini and grate them carefully into a bowl with a cheese grater. Season with a little salt. Add the remaining olive oil and toss well with your hands.

6 Scatter the grated zucchini over the mini-focaccias.

7 **Ask an adult to help you** put the mini-focaccias into the preheated oven and bake for about 10–15 minutes. **Ask an adult to help you** test them—they should be firm and golden, and sound hollow when tapped on their bottoms!

8 Serve warm, or let cool on a wire rack.

little cheese & tomato pizzas
pizzette margherita

6½ oz mozzarella
salt and black pepper

For the sauce
1 onion
2 garlic cloves
3 tablespoons olive oil
14-oz can cherry tomatoes
2 teaspoons sugar
a small handful of fresh
    basil

For the bases
3¾ cups bread flour, plus
    extra to sprinkle
1 envelope (7 g) fast-acting
    dry yeast
1 tablespoon olive oil
¾ cup warm water
    (see Tip on page 30)
2 large baking sheets,
    dusted with flour

Makes 6

1 **Ask an adult to help you** make the sauce. Peel the onion and chop it finely. Peel the garlic cloves (see Tip on page 18) and crush them with a garlic crusher. Heat the olive oil in a saucepan and fry the onion and garlic over gentle heat for about 4–5 minutes, until everything is soft but not colored.

2 Add the canned tomatoes and sugar, then season with a little salt and black pepper. Let the sauce bubble for 10–15 minutes, until glossy and thick, then add the basil and let the mixture simmer gently for 5 minutes more. Remove from the heat and set aside.

3 In the meantime, **ask an adult to help you** preheat the oven to 425°F.

4 To make the bases, put the flour, yeast, and a pinch of salt into a bowl and stir well.

5 Stir in the olive oil and 1–2 tablespoons warm water. Put your hands right in the bowl and mix the ingredients with your fingers.

Keep adding warm water, a little at a time, until you get a soft but not sticky dough.

6 Sprinkle a little flour over a clean work surface, turn the dough out onto it, and knead for 5–10 minutes (see Tip on page 13). The dough should be very smooth and pliable.

7 Divide the dough into 6 pieces. Using a rolling pin, roll each piece into a circle about 4 inches in diameter and lay them on the prepared baking sheets. Spread a thin layer of tomato sauce on each crust.

8 Break the mozzarella into small nuggets and dot them evenly over the crusts.

9 **Ask an adult to help you** put the sheet into the oven. Bake the pizzas for 6–7 minutes, until the crusts are golden and the cheese is bubbling. Serve at once.

Pizzette—little pizzas—are a favorite snack all over Italy, and you can buy them freshly made from the baker to eat on the go. They're not so easy to find outside Italy, but the good news is that they're a cinch to make at home!

Italy is shaped like a big, long boot that looks like it's kicking a ball. The "ball" is a beautiful island called Sardinia where they make this crunchy parchment bread. It's so thin that it looks like a sheet of music, hence the Italian name "carta di musica." Not only is it delicious, it's also fun to make because it doesn't need yeast and so it doesn't have to be left to rise like most breads. You need to roll the dough so thinly that you can almost see through it—or, if you don't mind having long pieces instead of circles, you could cheat a little and put it through a pasta machine. Make sure an adult is on hand to turn the bread halfway through the cooking—a pair of tongs is useful for this.

crunchy sardinian parchment bread
carta di musica

2 cups plus 2 tablespoons all-purpose flour, plus extra to sprinkle

1 cup fine semolina

1 teaspoon salt

1½ tablespoons finely chopped fresh rosemary

1¼ cups warm water (see Tip on page 30)

2 large baking sheets, dusted with flour

Makes 10–12

1 **Ask an adult to help you** preheat the oven to 425°F.

2 Put the flour, semolina, salt, and rosemary into a bowl and mix thoroughly.

3 Pour in 1–2 tablespoons warm water. Put your hands right in the bowl and mix the ingredients with your fingers. Keep adding warm water, a little at a time, until you get a soft but not sticky dough.

4 Sprinkle a little flour over a clean work surface, turn the dough out onto it, and knead for 2–3 minutes (see Tip on page 13). The dough should be very smooth and pliable.

5 Divide the dough into 10–12 pieces. Using a rolling pin, roll each piece out into large, roughly shaped wafer-thin circles.

6 Lay the circles on the prepared baking sheets (you will have to bake the bread in batches). **Ask an adult to help you** put the bread in the oven and bake for 2–3 minutes, until golden and puffy. Make sure the adult is the one to carefully turn the bread over. Bake it for a further 2 minutes. **Ask the adult to help you** remove the sheets from the oven. When the sheets and the bread have cooled, remove the bread and store in an airtight container until you are ready to eat it.

This is a lovely treat for breakfast and makes good use of fabulous summer plums. Choose plums which are sweet but not too soft, or they will ooze and make the bread soggy.

sweet plum focaccia
focaccia dolce con le prugne

3½ cups Italian "oo" type
   flour, plus extra to
   sprinkle
1 envelope (7 g) fast-acting
   dry yeast
a pinch of salt
½ cup sugar
4 tablespoons butter
about ¾ cup warm water
   (see Tip on page 30)

For the topping
3–4 ripe but firm plums
1 tablespoon sugar
a rectangular baking sheet,
   8 x 12 inches, dusted
   with flour

Makes one loaf

1 Put the flour, yeast, salt, and sugar into a bowl and stir well.

2 **Ask an adult to help you** melt the butter in a small saucepan.

3 Stir the melted butter into the bowl with the flour mixture. Pour in 1–2 tablespoons warm water. Put your hands right in the bowl and mix the ingredients with your fingers. Keep adding warm water, a little at a time, until you get a soft but not sticky dough.

4 Sprinkle a little flour over a clean work surface, turn the dough out onto it, and knead for 5–10 minutes (see Tip on page 13). The dough should be very smooth and pliable.

5 Using a rolling pin, roll the dough out into a rectangle slightly smaller than the prepared baking sheet. Lift it carefully into the sheet, cover with a clean kitchen towel, and let rise

in a warm place until the dough is double the original size.

6 **Ask an adult to help you** preheat the oven to 400°F.

7 **Ask an adult to help you** slice the plums in half and remove the pits. Cut the plums into thin slices and dab them on some paper towels to remove any extra juice. Push them gently but firmly into the top of the focaccia— either in neat lines or randomly, but in a single even layer.

8 Scatter over the sugar and **ask an adult to help you** transfer the sheet to the preheated oven. Bake the bread for about 25 minutes. **Ask an adult to help you** test that the bread is ready; it should be golden and firm, and the base should sound hollow when it is tapped.

9 Serve warm or at room temperature.

This baked polenta makes a lovely entrée for vegetarians, but is also nice served with meat as a change from potatoes. Alternatively, try it with the tomato sauce used for the tuna balls in the recipe on page 75.

baked polenta with cheese
polenta grigliata alla formaggio

4 cups vegetable broth
1½ cups instant polenta
1 cup freshly grated
  Parmesan
2 handfuls of baby spinach,
  torn
6½ tablespoons butter,
  softened
3½ oz Taleggio cheese
  (in one piece)
sunflower oil, to grease
salt and black pepper
a baking sheet
a cookie cutter (optional)
a large ovenproof dish

Serves 4

1 Pour the broth into a large, heavy saucepan, then **ask an adult to help you** turn on the heat. Let the broth heat up until it is bubbling nicely. Pour in the polenta in a steady stream, stirring quickly all the time with a large wire whisk. Do it gently so that it doesn't splash. Cook the polenta for the time recommended on the package you are using (some are quicker to cook than others).

2 When the polenta is cooked and thick, remove it from the heat and pop it on a heatproof work surface. Use an oven mitt to hold the saucepan handle. Swap the whisk for a wooden spoon and stir in the Parmesan, spinach, a little pepper, and half the butter. Have a little try (making sure it's not too hot first!) and see how it tastes. Add a little salt if you think it needs it.

3 Put a little sunflower oil on a paper towel and wipe it over the baking sheet to oil it.

4 **Ask an adult to help you** pour the mixture out onto the baking sheet, then smooth it over with a palette knife. Let cool and set.

5 **Ask an adult to help you** preheat the oven to 400°F.

6 Cut the polenta into circles using a cookie cutter or an upside-down glass and lay the circles in the ovenproof dish. **Ask an adult to help you** chop the cheese into little pieces, then dot the cheese evenly over the circles of polenta. Dot the remaining butter over too.

7 **Ask an adult to help you** bake the polenta in the preheated oven for about 15–20 minutes, until the cheese is melted and bubbling.

Polenta is very similar to semolina and makes a lovely pudding. You can serve this dessert as soon as it is cooked but I think it's lovely when left to set and baked with butter and sugar. Because you are using the zest of the orange, try to buy an unwaxed orange so that you don't end up eating waxy peel.

sweet polenta pudding
polenta dolce

2¹/₂ cups milk

1 large unwaxed orange

1³/4 cups instant polenta

²/₃ cup sugar, plus
    2 tablespoons for
    the topping

¹/₃ cup mixed candied peel

²/₃ cup candied orange peel

²/₃ cup golden raisins

3 tablespoons salted butter,
    plus 2 tablespoons
    for the topping

2 eggs

sunflower oil, to grease

light cream, to serve

a baking sheet

a cookie cutter (optional)

*a large ovenproof
    serving dish*

Serves 4

1 Pour 2¹/₂ cups water and the milk into a large saucepan and **ask an adult to help you** turn on the heat to medium. Bring it to a boil.

2 In the meantime, **ask an adult to help you** grate the orange zest (see Tip on page 24).

3 Pour the polenta in a steady stream into the saucepan with the water and milk, stirring quickly all the time with a large wire whisk. Do it gently so that it doesn't splash. Cook the polenta for the time recommended on the package.

4 When the polenta is cooked and thick, remove it from the heat and pop it on a heatproof work surface. Use an oven mitt to hold the saucepan handle. Swap the whisk for a wooden spoon and stir in the sugar, peel, raisins, grated orange zest, and butter. Stir until everything is evenly mixed and the butter has melted and been absorbed.

5 **Ask an adult to help you** crack the eggs into a small bowl and beat them until smooth.

6 Stir them into the polenta until everything is well mixed.

7 Put a little sunflower oil on a paper towel and wipe it over the baking sheet to oil it.

8 **Ask an adult to help you** pour the mixture out onto the baking sheet, then smooth it over with a palette knife. Let cool and set.

9 When you are ready to cook the polenta, **ask an adult to help you** preheat the oven to 400°F.

10 Cut the polenta into circles using a cookie cutter or an upside-down glass and lay the circles in the ovenproof serving dish.

11 To make the topping, **ask an adult to help you** melt the remaining butter in a saucepan. Drizzle the melted butter and the remaining sugar over the top of the polenta circles.

12 **Ask an adult to help you** transfer the dish to the preheated oven and bake the polenta for about 15–20 minutes, until golden. Serve with light cream.

By now, I think you'll have got the idea about just how much the Italians love to sit around the table and eat and drink and chat together! They don't hang around waiting for their food though; they want to get into the all-important business of eating straightaway! So first the bread goes on the table, and then, probably hot on the heels, a selection of antipasti (which means "before the meal") will follow. There are lots of different things that might be served—anything from a simple bowl of olives, a plate of salami, or some nice cheeses, to more complicated fare.

This section includes some ideas for antipasti and simple lunches, as well as some tasty snacks for the growling tummy times that might crop up now and again.

antipasti, easy lunches & snacks

tomato & bread soup
pappa al pomodoro

1³/4 lb ripe tomatoes
4 garlic cloves
6¹/2 oz stale, country-style
   bread
¹/4 cup olive oil, plus extra
   to drizzle
³/4 cup chicken or vegetable
   broth
6–7 fresh basil leaves, torn
salt and black pepper
freshly grated Parmesan,
   to serve

Serves 4

1 Ask an adult to help you make a little slice in each tomato with the point of a knife. Put the tomatoes into a large, heatproof bowl.

2 Ask an adult to help you boil the kettle and pour the boiling water over the tomatoes until they are covered. Leave them for 3–4 minutes.

3 In the meantime, **ask an adult to help you** peel the garlic cloves (see Tip on page 18) and cut them into thin slices, then cut the bread into small chunks.

4 After 3–4 minutes, the tomato skins should have started to curl away from the tomatoes. Carefully drain off the water, rinse them in cold water to cool them down a little, and, when you're sure they're cool enough to handle, peel the skin away.

5 Put the skinned tomatoes on a cutting board and cut them in half. Give them a squeeze to remove the seeds, then chop the tomato flesh roughly. Put into a saucepan.

6 Ask an adult to help you cook the soup, because you will need to work at the stovetop all the way through the rest of the recipe.

7 Heat the olive oil in a skillet and fry the bread chunks over medium heat for about 2–3 minutes, until light golden.

8 Stir in the tomatoes and garlic and cook for 5 minutes or so, until the tomatoes are starting to look a little sticky.

9 Pour in the broth and torn basil leaves and cook for about 20 minutes more, until the liquid has reduced and the soup is pulpy.

10 Have a little try of the soup and add a little salt and black pepper to taste. Stir well.

11 Remove the pan from the heat and set aside to cool a little.

12 Serve with some olive oil drizzled over the top and freshly grated Parmesan sprinkled over too.

This soup is very popular in the Tuscany region of Italy, and if you like tomatoey things, you'll love it. You can serve it hot, or at room temperature. I like it at room temperature with a good drizzle of extra virgin olive oil over the top. If you can't get really good, juicy, ripe tomatoes, use two 14-oz cans of cherry tomatoes, pop them in a colander, and rinse away the juice.

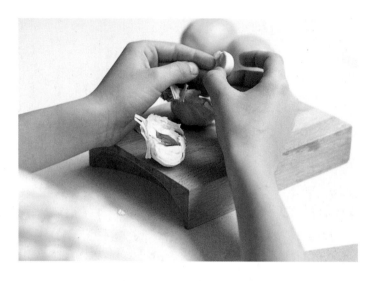

This is creamy and dreamy and you can make it with frozen peas, so it's quick as well as delicious!

creamy pea soup
crema di piselli

1 small onion
1 small potato (about 3 oz)
1 garlic clove
3 tablespoons olive oil
5 cups peas (fresh or
    frozen)
4 cups vegetable or
    chicken broth
3 tablespoons heavy cream
salt and black pepper
3 tablespoons olive oil,
    to drizzle
crusty bread, to serve

Serves 4

1 Ask an adult to help you prepare the vegetables. Peel the onion and chop it into fairly small pieces. Peel the potato and chop it into small, even-size pieces. Peel the garlic clove (see Tip on page 18) and crush it with a garlic crusher.

2 Ask an adult to help you heat the olive oil in a large saucepan, then add the onion, garlic, and potato. Cook over gentle heat for about 8–10 minutes, stirring quite often, until the onion is shiny and the potatoes are starting to soften.

3 Pour in the peas and the broth.

4 Let the soup simmer for about 20 minutes, until the potato is very soft—the potatoes should easily be squashed when you press them with a wooden spoon.

5 Ask an adult to help you remove the saucepan from the heat and purée the soup with a stick blender until it is smooth.

6 If you don't have a stick blender and are using a food processor or blender, you must let the soup cool a little before you blend it. Very hot soup can expand in the machine and may cause a nasty burn if you fill the machine too full.

7 Once the soup is nice and smooth, stir in the cream and season to taste with a little salt and some black pepper.

8 Spoon the mixture into pretty mugs or soup bowls, garnish with a drizzle of olive oil, and serve with some good crusty bread.

These are crunchy and munchy and make a great snack if you're ravenous when you come in from school. Cut the bread diagonally, to give long, nicely shaped slices.

tomato toasts
crostini di pomodori

1 small ciabatta loaf
½ cup olive oil
4 ripe tomatoes
2 garlic cloves
a handful of fresh parsley
 leaves
salt and black pepper
2 baking sheets

Serves 4

1 **Ask an adult to help you** preheat the oven to 400°F.

2 **Ask an adult to help you** cut the bread diagonally into thin slices. Put them on baking sheets and drizzle them with a little olive oil. Bake in the preheated oven for 5–10 minutes, until crisp and golden.

3 In the meantime, **ask an adult to help you** slice the tomatoes in half and remove the core at the top. Chop the flesh roughly and put it into a bowl.

4 Peel the garlic cloves (see Tip on page 18), crush them with a garlic crusher, then put into the bowl with the tomatoes. Season with salt and black pepper and the remaining olive oil.

5 **Ask an adult to help you** chop the parsley leaves and stir into the bowl of tomatoes.

6 **Ask an adult to help you** remove the hot baking sheets from the oven, then pile the mixture onto the toasts and serve.

These garlicky toasts make a great snack but you could also serve them alongside lots of other dishes. I think they taste much better than the usual garlic bread.

crispy garlic & olive oil toasts
fettunta

1 small ciabatta loaf
a handful of fresh parsley
  leaves
2–3 garlic cloves, halved
about ½ cup olive oil
coarse salt
2 baking sheets

Serves 4

1 **Ask an adult to help you** preheat the oven to 400°F.

2 **Ask an adult to help you** cut the bread diagonally into thin slices. Put them on baking sheets and bake them in the preheated oven for 5 minutes, until crisp and golden.

3 In the meantime, **ask an adult to help you** chop the parsley leaves.

4 **Ask an adult to help you** remove the hot baking sheets from the oven.

5 Rub the toasts all over with the cut surface of the garlic.

6 Drizzle a little olive oil over each toast, scatter over a tiny pinch of salt, sprinkle with the parsley, and serve.

little savory scones
bignè al formaggio

3 tablespoons butter
2 cups self-rising flour
a pinch of salt
½ cup freshly grated
  Parmesan
⅔ cup milk
1 small egg

For the filling
1 celery rib
3–4 fresh chives
3½ oz squacquerone, or
  other soft, creamy cheese
a cookie cutter (optional)
a baking sheet
a pastry brush

Makes 8

More fillings to try
3½ oz soft cheese and
  2 slices of prosciutto,
  chopped
3½ oz hard cheese, grated,
  and 1 chopped tomato
2 boiled eggs, mashed and
  mixed with 1 teaspoon
  snipped fresh chives
a small can of tuna in olive
  oil, drained and mixed
  with ½ small chopped
  onion and 1 small
  chopped tomato

1 **Ask an adult to help you** preheat the oven to 400°F.

2 **Ask an adult to help you** cut the butter into cubes. Put them in a bowl and sift over the flour and salt.

3 Put your hands in the bowl and rub the butter and flour together between your fingers and thumbs until the mixture looks like very fine bread crumbs.

4 Stir in the Parmesan.

5 Start pouring in the milk, a little at a time. Keep mixing everything with your hands and adding milk until you have a soft but not sticky dough.

The Italians have a lovely soft cheese called squacquerone (pronounced skwok-er-o-nee), which is irresistible. If you can't find it, use cream cheese for this recipe instead, or choose your own favorite creamy cheese.

6 Sprinkle a little flour over a clean work surface and turn the dough out onto it. Using a rolling pin, roll it gently into a circle about 1 inch thick.

7 Cut the dough into rounds using a cookie cutter or a small, upside-down glass and lay the circles on a baking sheet, leaving a little space between each.

8 Crack the egg into a small bowl, add 1 tablespoon water, and beat lightly with a fork until it's well mixed. This is an egg wash.

9 Using a pastry brush, paint the tops of the scones with the egg wash. This will make the scones nice and glossy when they're baked.

10 **Ask an adult to help you** transfer the sheet to the preheated oven and bake the scones for about 8–10 minutes, until they are firm and golden. Remove them and let them cool on a wire rack.

11 In the meantime, **ask an adult to help you** trim the ends of the celery and pull off some of the nasty stringy bits from the outside. Chop the celery finely. Snip the chives into pieces with kitchen scissors. Put the squacquerone cheese in a bowl and mix in the celery and chives.

12 Carefully cut the scones in half and spread some of the cheesy filling on each cut side.

little fried mozzarella & tomato sandwiches
mozzarella in carrozza

16 small, thin slices
of bread
3–4 tomatoes
6½ oz mozzarella cheese,
broken up into little
pieces with your fingers
3 eggs
3 tablespoons olive oil,
to fry
salt and black pepper

Serves 4

1 **Ask an adult to help you** cut the crusts off the bread and thinly slice the tomatoes.

2 Dot the mozzarella over 8 of the bread slices and lay the slices of tomato over the top. Top with the remaining bread slices and press lightly to seal.

3 Crack the eggs into a bowl, then beat with a fork until they are nice and smooth. Pour them into a shallow container in which you can fit the sandwiches. Lay the sandwiches in the egg and leave them for 2–3 minutes to soak up the egg. Turn them over and leave them for another 2–3 minutes so that the other side is soaked in egg too.

4 **Ask an adult to help you** fry the sandwiches. You will more than likely have to cook them in at least 2 batches, depending on the size of the skillet you have.

5 Heat a little of the olive oil in a nonstick skillet and fry the sandwiches on one side for about 3 minutes, until the bread is golden. Carefully turn the sandwiches over and fry for a further 2–3 minutes, until that side is golden too; the cheese inside should be well melted.

6 **Ask an adult to help you** remove the sandwiches from the skillet, cut them in half diagonally, and serve them straightaway.

These are lovely because they are crisp and eggy on the outside and gooey and creamy on the inside. They are a popular snack all over Italy. Add slices of ham if you like.

Pinzimonio is often served in restaurants as a nibble while you are waiting for dinner but sometimes, if you're having a long, very rich meal, it's offered partway through to freshen the appetite. A variety of raw vegetables is served in a bowl over ice to keep it fresh, then everyone dips them into really delicious olive oil. It makes a refreshing alternative to heavier cream- or cheese-based dips. You must use a good extra virgin olive oil though!

little tomato cups with olive oil & crunchy vegetable dippers
pinzimonio in coppette di pomodoro

1 carrot
1 small celery rib
1 small red bell pepper
1 small yellow bell pepper
a small handful of fine
    green beans
4 vine-ripened tomatoes
1/3 cup olive oil
salt and black pepper

Serves 4

1 Wash all the vegetables well.

2 **Ask an adult to help you** prepare the vegetables. Trim the carrot and peel it with a vegetable peeler. Cut it into thin sticks or fingers, each about 2 inches long.

3 **Ask an adult to help you** trim the ends of the celery and pull off some of the nasty stringy bits from the outside. Cut it into pieces roughly the same size as the carrots.

4 Cut the bell peppers in half, scrape out the seeds, and remove the stalks. Cut the flesh into thin sticks or fingers too.

5 Trim the green beans and cut them in half to make them a similar size to the bell peppers and carrots.

6 To keep the vegetables fresh and crisp, pop them into a bowl of ice-cold water until you are ready to eat them.

7 Meanwhile, cut the tops carefully off the tomatoes. Using a teaspoon, scoop out the seeds and core of each tomato, taking care not to damage the sides of the tomato or make any holes. Make sure you leave it nice and clean inside.

8 Lay the tomatoes in the center of a pretty platter and sprinkle the tiniest pinch of salt in each.

9 Carefully pour in enough olive oil to come two-thirds the way up the tomato cups.

10 Arrange the vegetable sticks nicely around the tomato cups and serve.

This recipe makes A LOT of bread sticks but the amount really depends how thick and how long you make them. Don't worry, they freeze very well and can be crisped up in the oven when required.

parmesan bread sticks

grissini con parmigiano

3³/4 cups bread flour, plus extra to sprinkle

1 envelope (7 g) fast-acting dry yeast

1 teaspoon salt

1 tablespoon olive oil

about ³/4 cup warm water (see Tip on page 30)

1 cup freshly grated Parmesan

2 large baking sheets, dusted with flour

Makes ... oodles!

1 Ask an adult to help you preheat the oven to 425°F.

2 Put the flour, yeast, and salt in a bowl and stir well. Stir in the olive oil and just 1–2 tablespoons warm water. Put your hands right in the bowl and mix the ingredients with your fingers. Keep adding warm water, a little at a time, until you have a soft but not sticky dough.

3 Scatter the Parmesan over the bread and knead well, until all the cheese has been mixed into the dough.

4 Sprinkle a little flour over a clean work surface, turn the dough out onto it, and knead for 5–10 minutes (see Tip on page 13). The dough should be very smooth and elastic.

5 Break off pieces of dough about the size of large walnuts and roll into long sticks using your hands. Lay the bread sticks on the prepared baking sheets.

6 Ask an adult to help you put the bread sticks in the preheated oven and bake for 5 minutes, until golden and crisp. Remove from the oven and let cool on wire racks.

Almost as soon as you sit down in a restaurant in Italy, you'll be offered bread, shortly followed by a plate of scrumptious things to nibble on and get your appetite going for what's to come. All these nibbles are called antipasti. If you're planning to make a special meal, an antipasti platter is an easy way to serve a appetizer and it's especially nice because it's very relaxed—you can make it well ahead of time, and then when the meal starts, you can just let everyone chat away and help themselves. Take a pretty platter and build a selection from the following ideas.

antipasti platter

ITALIAN MEATS
The Italians make a lot of different cured meats ("cured" means that they are preserved by marinating in herbs or spices and then dried in the mountain air for a long time to preserve them, rather than being cooked). Some typical kinds are salami (cured pork with spices), prosciutto di Parma (cured pork from Parma in northern Italy), speck (another kind of cured pork), San Daniele ham (like Parma ham) and bresaola (very thin slices of cured beef).

BREADSTICKS WITH PROSCIUTTO
Make a batch of the bread sticks on the page opposite. Buy some prosciutto and cut the slices into 3 strips. Wrap a strip around the top of each bread stick.

SUN-DRIED TOMATOES
Buy sun-dried tomatoes preserved in olive oil and drain them, then spear them onto toothpicks. They're especially good if you add a little cube of crumbly cheese, such as Parmesan, or even tiny little balls of mozzarella called bocconcini (see right).

SLICES OF ITALIAN CHEESE
If your local supermarket has a good cheese or deli counter, have a look for Italian cheeses such as Provolone, Asiago, Fontina, or pecorino, although you could always cheat and use some cheeses from other countries too! All you need to do is slice them thinly and arrange them in an attractive way on a pretty platter.

LITTLE NUGGETS OF PARMESAN
All you have to do is carefully dig out little nuggets of Parmesan with a knife and spear them with toothpicks, ready for picking up.

BOCCONCINI
Bocconcini are little bite-size balls of mozzarella cheese. Add a little pile to your platter and put some toothpicks nearby for people to help themselves.

OLIVES
Choose green olives if you like them tangy and firm and black if you prefer them softer and oilier. Even if you're not keen on them at all, keep trying—you might grow to like them. And don't forget that your guests might love them!

Although in modern Italy meals no longer involve quite as many courses as they would in days gone by (unless it's a particular time of the year such as Christmas or a special celebration), very often in Italy you can expect to eat as much as an antipasti course, followed by a bowl of pasta, and then a meat or fish dish as an entrée—not forgetting dessert at the end. Of course, you could do the same and serve the dishes in the following section after two courses and before the sweet, but you might like to serve slightly smaller portions! In any case, there is a good selection to suit either a weekday meal or a special occasion to impress family and friends.

entrées

This is really easy and tasty. It goes really well with the tomato sauce on page 75 and the rosemary potatoes on page 82.

meatloaf
polpettone

1 onion

2 garlic cloves

1 egg

2 lb lean ground beef

2 teaspoons dried oregano

1 ½ cups freshly grated Parmesan

salt and black pepper

Tomato Sauce (page 75), to serve

Rosemary Potatoes (page 82), to serve

a 5 x 9-inch loaf pan

Serves 4

1 Put the loaf pan on a sheet of parchment paper and draw around the base. Cut out the rectangle and lay it in the bottom of the pan to line it.

2 Ask an adult to help you preheat the oven to 350°F.

3 Ask an adult to help you peel and chop the onion into quite small pieces. Peel the garlic cloves (see Tip on page 18) and crush them with a garlic crusher. Put the onion and garlic into a large bowl.

4 Crack the egg into a bowl and beat with a fork until smooth. Pour into the bowl with the onion and garlic along with the ground beef, oregano, and Parmesan.

5 Season well with salt and black pepper.

6 Mix the ingredients with a wooden spoon until everything is well combined.

7 Spoon the mixture into the loaf pan and smooth the top with the back of a spoon.

8 Ask an adult to help you transfer the pan to the preheated oven and cook for 45 minutes.

9 Ask an adult to help you remove the pan from the oven and turn the meatloaf out onto a cutting board. Cut in slices and serve with Tomato Sauce and Rosemary Potatoes.

easy pea, sausage & onion calzone
calzone con piselli, salsiccia e cipolla

8 oz Italian sausage links
1 onion
2 garlic cloves
2 ripe tomatoes
6 tablespoons olive oil
1 cup frozen peas, thawed
4 small flour tortillas
3 tablespoons mascarpone
1 small egg
salt and black pepper
a pastry brush

Serves 4

1 Ask an adult to help you cut away the skins of the sausages with kitchen scissors and throw the skins away. Pull the sausage meat into chunks, put in a bowl, and set aside.

2 Ask an adult to help you peel the onion and chop it finely. Peel the garlic cloves (see Tip on page 18) and crush them with a garlic crusher.

3 Ask an adult to help you slice the top off the tomatoes and squeeze out the seeds. Chop the flesh into small pieces.

4 Ask an adult to help you heat 3 tablespoons of the olive oil in a saucepan and fry the onion and garlic over gentle heat for 3–4 minutes, until the onion is starting to soften.

5 Add the sausage meat and season with salt and black pepper. Cook for 1–2 minutes longer, until the sausage meat is golden. Give it all a good stir every once in a while.

6 Add the tomatoes and peas to the pan. Stir well and cook for another 15 minutes or so, until all the liquid has disappeared, the meat is cooked, and the mixture is deliciously sticky.

7 Lay the tortillas out on a cutting board and spoon one-quarter of the mixture onto one side of each tortilla, leaving a 1-inch border around the edges. Dot little bits of mascarpone over the sausage-meat mixture.

8 Crack the egg into a bowl and beat with a fork until smooth.

9 Brush some beaten egg around the edge of the tortillas with a pastry brush. Fold over each tortilla to make a semi-circle shape. Press the edges down to seal them.

10 Ask an adult to help you heat the remaining oil in a large skillet over medium heat and fry the tortillas for 3–4 minutes on each side, until golden. Drain on paper towels.

Calzone are a bit like hot sandwiches made from pizza dough. Although in my recipe they are made with flour tortillas, they taste every bit as good and are lighter and quicker to make.

There isn't much to say about this easy tart
—it's just too delicious for words!

upside-down cheese & tomato tart
sfogliata al formaggio e pomodoro

½ slice of stale white bread

5 oz Provolone cheese

14 oz cherry tomatoes

2 tablespoons olive oil,
   plus extra to grease

all-purpose flour,
   to sprinkle

10 oz puff pastry dough,
   thawed if frozen

salt and black pepper

a crisp, green salad,
   to serve

*a 9-inch loose-bottomed
   tart pan*

Serves 4

1 **Ask an adult to help you** preheat the oven to 400°F.

2 Put a little olive oil on a paper towel and wipe the base of the tart pan with it to oil it.

3 **Ask an adult to help you** whiz the bread in a food processor until you get crumbs. Scatter over the bottom of the tart pan.

4 **Ask an adult to help you** cut the cheese into small, thin slices and arrange them over the bread crumbs. Scatter the tomatoes over the cheese slices, drizzle with the olive oil, and season with salt and black pepper.

5 Sprinkle a little flour over a clean work surface and put the puff pastry dough on it. Using a rolling pin, roll it gently into a circle slightly larger than the tart pan.

6 Lay the pastry over the tomatoes and tuck the edges into the pan.

7 **Ask an adult to help you** put the tart into the preheated oven and bake for about 25 minutes, until the pastry is golden brown and risen.

8 **Ask an adult to help you** remove the tart from the oven and let cool for about 5 minutes, until it is cool enough to handle safely with oven mitts on.

9 **Ask an adult to help you** place an upturned dinner plate (larger than the tart pan) over the pan. Carefully flip everything over so that the plate is on the bottom. Pull the pan away and the tart should slip out onto the plate. The tomatoes will be on top now and the cheese should be lovely and melted. Serve in slices, with a crisp, green salad.

salmon on sticks
spiedini di salmone

20 oz salmon fillet
a small bunch of fresh
    chives
freshly squeezed juice of
    ½ small lemon
salt
1 lb cherry tomatoes
3 tablespoons olive oil
lemon wedges, to serve
Tomato & Bread Salad
    (page 89), to serve
    (optional)
12 wooden skewers,
    about 12 inches long
a ridged stovetop grill pan
a pastry brush

Makes about 12

1 Soak the skewers in a dish of cold water for 30 minutes. This will stop them burning when you put them on the hot grill pan.

2 Meanwhile, **ask an adult to help you** cut the salmon into bite-size chunks. Snip the chives into pieces with kitchen scissors.

3 Pop the salmon, lemon juice, and chives in a large bowl and season with a little salt.

4 Push a chunk of salmon onto a skewer and then a tomato. Continue pushing alternate pieces of salmon and tomato onto skewers until you run out of salmon and tomatoes (leave 2 inches at the end of the skewers).

5 **Ask an adult to help you** heat a ridged stovetop grill pan until quite hot. Brush the olive oil over the skewers with a pastry brush. Lay them on the hot grill pan and cook for about 5–6 minutes, until the salmon is cooked through and golden brown. Turn them over once halfway through cooking. You will need to cook them in batches.

6 Serve with lemon wedges to squeeze over. You might like to try it with the Tomato & Bread Salad.

Spiedini are very popular in Italy —they are skewers of meat or fish and vegetables, very similar to kabobs. These salmon spiedini are especially tasty cooked on an outdoor grill in the summer, but you can cook them just as easily on a stovetop grill pan too.

Arrosticini are very famous in the area of Italy where I live—they even have special grills to cook them on that look like long, thin trough-shaped barbecues. Arrosticini are made from tiny cubes of mutton threaded onto skewers and the special grill is designed so that the ends of the skewers don't sit over the heat and burn. For this recipe, I've used little squares of lamb, and with some adult help, you can easily cook them on a stovetop grill pan or an outdoor grill—they're incredibly easy to make and far too tasty not to try!

abruzzese-style lamb skewers
arrosticini

1 lb lamb fillet
salt
tomato salad, to serve
Rosemary Potatoes
    (page 82), to serve
30 wooden skewers,
    about 12 inches long

Makes about 30

1 Soak the skewers in a dish of cold water for 30 minutes. This will stop them burning when you put them on the hot grill pan.

2 Meanwhile, **ask an adult to help you** cut the lamb into small bite-size chunks.

3 Push the pieces of lamb onto the skewers until you run out of lamb (leave 2 inches at each end of the skewers).

4 Season the lamb with salt.

5 **Ask an adult to help you** heat a ridged stovetop grill pan until hot. Lay the skewers on the pan and cook for 10 minutes, until the lamb is cooked through and dark brown. Turn them over once halfway through cooking. You will need to cook them in batches.

6 Serve with a tomato salad and some Rosemary Potatoes.

Frittatas are eaten all over Italy. They're a little bit like flat omelets. They're often cooked on the stovetop and finished off under the broiler, but this one is easier because it's simply baked in the oven. It's made with pieces of Italian bacon (pancetta, see page 9) and sweet leeks, but you could try other vegetables — zucchini, onions, mushrooms, peas, tomatoes, beans—and even add your favorite grated cheese too.

leek frittata
frittata con porri

3 leeks
3½ oz pancetta, cut into
   matchsticks
2 tablespoons olive oil
8 extra-large eggs
a few fresh chives
salt and black pepper
a crisp, green salad,
   to serve
a round ovenproof dish
   with a diameter of about
   9 inches

Serves 4

1 **Ask an adult to help you** preheat the oven to 400°F.

2 **Ask an adult to help you** trim off the bottom of the leeks and cut off any thick, dark leaves at the top. Cut the leeks in half along their length and wash them very well—sometimes grit can get caught between the leaves.

3 Cut the leeks into fine slices and scatter them over the base of the ovenproof dish.

4 Scatter over the pancetta pieces and drizzle with the olive oil.

5 **Ask an adult to help you** pop the dish in the preheated oven and roast for about 15 minutes, until the pancetta is cooked and the leeks are softened.

6 In the meantime, crack the eggs into a bowl and beat with a wire whisk until very smooth. Season with salt and black pepper.

7 **Ask an adult to help you** remove the hot dish from the oven and put it on a heatproof surface. Carefully pour in the eggs, taking care not to touch the hot dish.

8 Snip the chives into pieces with kitchen scissors and scatter over the frittata.

9 **Ask an adult to help you** return the dish to the oven and bake for about 20 minutes longer, until the eggs are set.

10 **Ask an adult to help you** take the dish out of the oven. Serve with a crisp, green salad. You can serve it warm or cold, if you prefer.

These tasty little fish balls are so simple to make and the great thing is that everything you need can probably be found in your kitchen cupboard, making them a great standby if you have unexpected visitors for lunch! Try to use tuna packed in olive oil, or at the very least in sunflower oil—it's tastier, has a better texture and is healthier than the tuna packed in water.

cheese & tuna fish balls with tomato sauce
polpettine al tonno con salsa di pomodoro

4–5 tablespoons olive oil
salt and black pepper

For the tuna fish balls
2 thick slices of white bread, crusts removed
two 8-oz cans tuna in olive oil, drained
1 egg
1½ cups grated sharp cheddar cheese

For the tomato sauce
1 onion
2 garlic cloves
3 tablespoons olive oil
14-oz can tomatoes
2 teaspoons sugar
a small handful of fresh basil leaves, torn (or ½ teaspoon dried oregano)

Serves 4

1 To make the tuna fish balls, **ask an adult to help you** cut the crusts off the bread and whiz the bread in a food processor until you get crumbs. Transfer the bread crumbs to a bowl with the tuna and stir until well mixed.

2 Crack the egg into the bowl, then add the cheese. Season with salt and black pepper.

3 Take a small amount of the tuna mixture in your hands and roll it around between your palms to make a walnut-size ball. Repeat with the rest of the mixture until there is none left. Set the fish balls aside.

4 To make the tomato sauce, **ask an adult to help you** peel the onion and chop it finely. Peel the garlic cloves (see Tip on page 18) and crush them with a garlic crusher.

5 Ask an adult to help you heat the olive oil in a saucepan and fry the onion and garlic over gentle heat for 4–5 minutes, until the onion has softened but not colored.

6 Add the canned tomatoes and sugar to the pan and season with a little salt and black pepper. Let the sauce bubble for about 10–15 minutes, until glossy and thick, then add the basil and let the mixture simmer gently for 5 minutes more.

7 Ask an adult to help you heat the olive oil in a skillet and fry the fish balls for about 4–5 minutes, until hot and golden. Transfer them to a dish and pour the tomato sauce over the top. Serve with pasta or potatoes and vegetables.

The Italians make fabulously meaty sausages and one of my favorites is called luganega. If you can't find these, just use regular Italian-style sausages. Don't worry about the whole cloves of garlic in this—when cooked this way, garlic is mild and delicious squashed onto the bread with the beans when you're eating it.

sausage & beans
salsicce con fagioli

2 red onions

1½ lb Italian-style sausages

3 tablespoons olive oil

4–5 garlic cloves

two 14-oz cans cherry tomatoes, drained and rinsed

1 cup vegetable or meat broth

1 dried bay leaf

14-oz can cannellini beans, drained and rinsed

a small handful of fresh parsley leaves

4 slices of country-style bread, toasted, to serve

an ovenproof casserole dish or deep roasting pan

Serves 4

1 Ask an adult to help you preheat the oven to 400°F.

2 Ask an adult to help you peel the onions, cut them in half, and slice each half thinly. Scatter them over the base of the ovenproof casserole dish or deep roasting pan.

3 Scatter the sausages over the onions and drizzle everything with the olive oil.

4 Ask an adult to help you transfer the dish to the preheated oven and roast for about 20 minutes, until the onions are soft and the sausages have started to color.

5 Ask an adult to help you take the dish out of the oven.

6 Peel the garlic cloves (see Tip on page 18) and scatter them whole over the sausages in the dish.

7 Add the canned tomatoes, broth, bay leaf, and beans. **Ask an adult to help you** return the dish to the oven. Bake for 30 minutes longer, until the onions are tender and the sausages are cooked through.

8 Ask an adult to help you remove the dish from the oven and chop the parsley leaves. Stir in all but a spoonful of the parsley.

9 Put a slice of bread in each of 4 bowls. Spoon the sausages and beans over the bread, and some of the sauce around. Scatter the remaining parsley over the top.

This dish doesn't make the prettiest sauce you'll ever come across but it may well be one of the tastiest! The chicken ends up fabulously juicy, and the milk and lemons bubble down to make sticky, citrussy nuggets. Tell everyone to squash the soft garlic out of its skin and smear it onto the meat too!

chicken poached in milk & lemons
pollo con latte e limone

2 small, unwaxed lemons
a 5-lb chicken
2 tablespoons olive oil
1 whole head of garlic,
  cloves separated but
  left unpeeled
a small bunch of fresh sage
4 cups milk
salt and black pepper
bread, to serve

Serves 6

1 Ask an adult to help you cut each lemon into 6 wedges.

2 Season the chicken. **Ask an adult to help you** heat half the olive oil in a large saucepan and cook the chicken, breast-side down, for 4–5 minutes, until golden. Turn the chicken over and cook for 3–4 minutes more.

3 Ask an adult to help you remove the chicken from the pan and pour away any used oil.

4 Pour the remaining olive oil into the pan and add the lemon wedges and garlic. Stir-fry for 2–3 minutes, until golden. Add the sage and cook for another minute or so.

5 Return the chicken to the pan and pour the milk over it.

6 Put a lid on the pan, leaving a little opening to allow for the steam to escape. Simmer over gentle heat for about 1 hour, until the meat is cooked through and the sauce has curdled into sticky nuggets (take care to keep the heat low, or the milk will reduce too quickly to fully cook the chicken).

7 Ask an adult to help you remove the pan from the heat. Let the chicken rest for about 4–5 minutes before slicing. Serve warm with the sauce and bread to mop up the sauce.

On the whole, Italians don't tend to serve a huge range of vegetables alongside the entrée—perhaps just one vegetable such as potatoes or maybe a salad and occasionally both. But they do have a wonderful way with them. Here is a selection of vegetables that should be easy to find anywhere. I hope these recipes will prove to you that vegetables don't have to be boring and that there's more to salad than just lettuce and tomatoes!

vegetables
& salads

Potatoes roasted with rosemary and garlic are heavenly.
They are the perfect accompaniment to a Sunday lunch.

rosemary potatoes
patate con rosmarino

2¼ lb Yukon Gold potatoes
4 tablespoons olive oil
2 garlic cloves
a small handful of fresh
   rosemary leaves
salt and black pepper

Serves 4

1 Ask an adult to help you preheat the oven to 400°F.

2 Ask an adult to help you peel the potatoes and cut them into small chunks. Put them in a bowl, cover with water, and let them soak for 10 minutes, then drain and pat dry on paper towels.

3 Pour the olive oil into a roasting pan and **ask an adult to help you** put it in the preheated oven. Heat for 3–4 minutes until the oil is hot.

4 Peel the garlic cloves (see Tip on page 18) and crush them with a garlic crusher.

5 Ask an adult to help you to remove the pan from the oven and carefully add the potatoes, taking care that the hot oil doesn't splash. Return the pan to the oven and roast the potatoes for about 35 minutes, until crisp and golden and almost soft.

6 Ask an adult to help you chop the rosemary.

7 Ask an adult to help you remove the pan from the oven and scatter the garlic, rosemary, and some salt and black pepper over the potatoes. Stir and return to the oven for 5–10 minutes longer. Drain the potatoes on paper towels before serving.

Broccoli is fine by itself, but don't you think it can seem a little bit boring sometimes? Well, try it the way the Italians often serve it, with a drizzle of olive oil and a scattering of crispy crumbs. Once upon a time, fried crumbs like this were used by peasants as a substitute for Parmesan cheese, because Parmesan was very expensive and the crumbs added a similar texture; now people just add the bread crumbs anyway because they taste so good!

broccoli with poor man's parmesan
broccolo con aglio e muddica

20 oz broccoli

Poor man's parmesan
2 garlic cloves
1 unwaxed lemon
2 tablespoons fresh parsley
  leaves
5–6 slices of white bread
4 tablespoons olive oil
salt and black pepper

Serves 4

1 Break the broccoli into small florets and put into a saucepan. Pour in enough water to cover the broccoli.

2 **Ask an adult to help you** put the pan on the stove over quite high heat. Bring to a boil.

3 Turn the heat down and simmer until the broccoli is almost soft but still has a little bite to it. **Ask an adult to help you** test it by pricking it gently with the tip of a sharp knife —it should feel quite soft but not so soft that it slips off the knife.

4 **Ask an adult to help you** drain the broccoli and transfer it to a dish to keep warm while you make the poor man's Parmesan.

5 Peel the garlic cloves (see Tip on page 18) and crush them with a garlic crusher.

6 Wash the lemon and **ask an adult to help you** grate the zest (see Tip on page 24) and to chop the parsley.

7 **Ask an adult to help you** whiz the bread in a food processor until you get crumbs. Transfer to a large bowl and stir in the garlic, lemon zest, parsley, and a little salt and black pepper.

8 **Ask an adult to help you** heat 2 tablespoons of the olive oil in a skillet and add the crumb mixture. Cook over gentle heat for about 2–3 minutes, until crisp and golden.

9 Drizzle over the remaining olive oil and scatter over the poor man's Parmesan.

Sweet peas, creamy eggs, and salty Parmesan cheese make a scrumptious mix; this is a lovely dish to serve with both meat and fish. My son Tim loves this; often he's happy to have a bowl for lunch with some bread.

eggy peas
piselli con parmigiano e uova

6 eggs
³/4 cup freshly grated Parmesan
3¹/2 cups frozen peas, thawed
2 tablespoons olive oil
salt and black pepper

Serves 4

1 Crack the eggs into a bowl and beat with a fork until smooth.

2 Stir in the grated Parmesan and the peas and season with salt and black pepper.

3 **Ask an adult to help you** heat the olive oil in a skillet, then carefully pour in the pea mixture and cook over medium heat, stirring all the time, until the eggs have cooked and the peas are coated.

These make such an easy and delicious side dish. If you like,
you could leave them without heating and serve them as a salad.

cannellini beans with garlic & parsley
fagioli con aglio e prezzemolo

1 small onion
4 tablespoons fresh parsley
  leaves
2 garlic cloves
two 14-oz cans cannellini
  beans, drained and
  rinsed
1/3 cup peppery olive oil,
  plus extra to serve
salt and black pepper

Serves 6

1 **Ask an adult to help you** peel the onion
and chop it finely, and to chop the parsley.
Peel the garlic cloves (see Tip on page 18)
and crush them with a garlic crusher.

2 Put the beans in a saucepan and add the
onion, garlic, olive oil, and half the parsley.

3 Season with salt and black pepper and stir
gently but thoroughly. Set aside for about
30 minutes to allow the flavors to develop.

4 **Ask an adult to help you** heat the beans
gently until warm. Stir in the remaining
parsley and drizzle with a little extra olive oil.

Panzanella is a lovely Italian salad usually made with a base of tomatoes and bread.

tomato & bread salad
panzanella

½ cup olive oil

1 stale ciabatta loaf

2 celery ribs, sliced

1 red onion

1 red bell pepper

8 oz tomatoes

1 small cucumber

2 garlic cloves

3 tablespoons red wine
  vinegar

a handful of fresh basil
  leaves, torn

salt and black pepper

a baking sheet

Serves 6

1 Ask an adult to help you preheat the oven to 400°F.

2 Ask an adult to help you cut the ciabatta into small chunks and put them on a baking sheet. Drizzle with 3 tablespoons of the olive oil, season with salt and black pepper, and stir well. Put in the preheated oven and bake for about 10 minutes until golden and crunchy.

3 Ask an adult to help you prepare the salad vegetables. Trim the ends of the celery and pull off some of the nasty stringy bits from the outside. Slice the celery and put it in a salad bowl.

4 Peel the onion and slice it thinly. Cut the bell pepper in half, scrape out the seeds, and remove the stalks. Cut the flesh into thin strips. Cut tomatoes in half. Cut the cucumber in half along its length and scoop out the seeds with a teaspoon, then cut the flesh into thin slices. Add everything to the salad bowl.

5 Peel the garlic cloves (see Tip on page 18) and crush them with a garlic crusher.

6 Mix the vinegar and garlic with the remaining olive oil and season to taste. Pour over the salad, add the roughly torn basil, and toss thoroughly, making sure that the ciabatta chunks get a good coating of the dressing.

7 Leave for an hour or so before serving if possible, to allow the flavors to develop and the bread to soften very slightly.

89

Leafy, crunchy salad greens simply tossed with a tasty dressing are hard to beat as an appetizer or side dish. Here are just a couple of suggestions for easy dressings to suit different types of salad, as well as the lowdown on which greens you might like.

a basic green salad

It's very easy to find bags of pre-mixed salads in the stores now, but it is much more fun if you can buy fresh greens and make your own. If you like sweet, crunchy greens, go for something like Romaine lettuce or an iceberg.

If you like something with a bit more oomph, go for peppery arugula, raw spinach, or curly endive. You may even like crisp young escarole—it has a slightly bitter taste but give it a try!

AN EASY CHEESEY SALAD DRESSING FOR SWEETER GREENS

This is a tiny bit like a Caesar salad dressing but it doesn't have any anchovies in it. It tastes lovely with crisp Romaine lettuce. Of course, if you happen to be an anchovy fan, you could always whiz in a couple with a handheld stick blender, or add a drop or two of Worcestershire sauce, which has an anchovy kick to it.

If you want to add a scattering of golden croutons on your salad, simply follow the recipe at the beginning of the Tomato & Bread Salad on page 89.

Put 4–5 tablespoons freshly grated Parmesan, 6 tablespoons mayonnaise, 2–3 tablespoons water, and 1 crushed garlic clove in a small bowl and stir well.

A BASIC SALAD DRESSING FOR DARKER OR MORE PEPPERY GREENS

Balsamic vinegar has a distinctive sweet flavor, so it makes a good match for greens with a strong taste. Baby spinach leaves are perfect with this dressing. Make some Parmesan shavings using a potato peeler and ask an adult to help you toast a few pine nuts.

Put 6 tablespoons extra virgin olive oil and 2 tablespoons balsamic vinegar in a small bowl and whisk.

Strictly speaking, Italians aren't big dessert eaters (it's hardly surprising when you think how many other courses there might be during one meal!) Desserts to follow lunch or dinner will very often consist of seasonal fruit, which isn't a bad thing at all considering the wonderful choice on offer throughout most of the year. They do make some great cakes and pastries, but these might be eaten at breakfast time or with coffee in the morning. Here are some of my favorites, and of course, you can choose to eat them at any time of the day!

One dessert the Italians are big fans of is ice cream—and they really do make the dreamiest ice cream. It takes real willpower to walk past a gelateria (ice-cream shop) on a hot summer's day without calling in to buy a cone or dish filled with irresistible, velvety-smooth gelato. The flavors available are out of this world! I realize that unless you're super lucky, hopping over to Italy just for an ice cream isn't very likely to be possible, so here are some lip-licking recipes that will bring Italy a little nearer to you.

sweets & ice cream

We buy moist little coconut cakes like this in our local pastry shop. They make a lovely sweet treat.

coconut kisses
baci di cocco

3 tablespoons butter,
    plus extra to grease
1⅓ cups desiccated
    coconut
¼ cup sugar
1 egg
a baking sheet

Makes about 10

1 **Ask an adult to help you** preheat the oven to 300°C. Put a little butter on a paper towel and rub it over the baking sheet to grease it.

2 **Ask an adult to help you** melt the butter in a small saucepan, then let cool for a while.

3 Put the coconut, sugar, and butter in a large bowl and stir until well mixed.

4 Crack the egg into a separate bowl and beat with a fork, then add to the other ingredients and stir well.

5 Take walnut-size amounts of the mixture in your hands and shape into small pyramids. Put on the baking sheet and **ask an adult to help you** transfer them to the oven. Bake for 15 minutes or so, until golden.

6 Transfer to a wire rack and let cool.

This is the sort of quick dessert that Italian children might have if their moms are busy—just as we might have a container of yogurt sometimes. Stir a pinch of ground cinnamon into the sugar if you like.

sugared ricotta with fresh fruit

1 lb chilled ricotta
2–3 tablespoons sugar
fresh fruit, to serve

Serves 4

1 Spoon the ricotta into dessert bowls and sprinkle the sugar over the top.

2 Serve with your favorite fresh fruit.

Delicious pancake parcels oozing with sweet, sticky mascarpone, honey, and pears—yum!

baked pancake parcels with pears & mascarpone

crespelle di pere e mascarpone

2 tablespoons butter,
   plus extra to grease

For the pancakes
2 tablespoons butter
2 eggs
1¼ cups milk
a pinch of salt
1 cup all-purpose flour,
   sifted

For the filling
1 lb mascarpone
3 ripe but firm pears
4 tablespoons dark honey
   (chestnut, if possible)
an ovenproof dish

Serves 4

1 To make the pancakes, **ask an adult to help you** melt the butter in a pan, then pour it into the bowl of a food processor or in a blender with the eggs and milk and whiz to combine.

2 Sift the salt and flour into the bowl and whiz until you have a smooth batter. Set aside for 30 minutes–1 hour.

3 **Ask an adult to help you** cook the pancakes. Put a little of the butter for frying in a small nonstick skillet or crêpe pan and heat over medium heat until hot. If the batter has thickened, you may need to add a little water.

4 Pour in a small amount of batter (just enough to cover the base of the skillet) and tilt the skillet to spread the mixture evenly. Cook for 1–2 minutes, until the pancake is golden on the underside and little bubbles have started to appear on the surface. Using a palette knife, loosen the pancake around the edges and turn it over. Cook for another minute, until golden brown.

5 Repeat until all the remaining batter has been used up—it should make 8 pancakes. Keep adding butter a little at a time between pancakes to keep the skillet greased.

6 Put the finished pancakes on top of a large sheet of aluminum foil and stack them between layers of parchment paper. Wrap up the foil and put the parcel in a low oven until you are ready to use the pancakes.

7 To make the filling, put the mascarpone in a large bowl and beat until smooth, then remove 3 tablespoons to another small bowl.

8 **Ask an adult to help you** peel the pears, remove the cores and cut the flesh into small pieces. Fold lightly into the large bowl of mascarpone. Fold in 2 tablespoons of the honey very lightly to give a rippled effect.

9 **Ask an adult to help you** preheat the broiler until hot. Put a little butter on a paper towel and rub it over the ovenproof dish to grease it. Remove the pancakes from the oven and lay one out flat on a cutting board. Spoon an eighth of the pear mixture onto the center. Fold into a flat parcel and put in the dish, seam-side down. Repeat with all the remaining pancakes.

10 Dot the remaining mascarpone over the parcels and drizzle over the last of the honey. Broil for 4 minutes until golden and bubbling.

Italian children love these pretty filled cookies; they usually come filled with jam or chocolate. I usually make some of each!

little filled flower cookies

6 tablespoons butter, softened
⅓ cup confectioners' sugar, plus extra to dust
1 egg yolk
1 cup all-purpose flour plus 2 tablespoons cake flour
jam or chocolate spread
2 baking sheets
2 cookie cutters, 2 inches and ½ inch

Makes 10

1 **Ask an adult to help you** preheat the oven to 350°F. Line the baking sheets with parchment paper.

2 Put the butter and sugar into a bowl and beat with a wooden spoon until smooth.

3 Add the egg yolk and beat again until it is well mixed in.

4 Stir in the flour and mix until you get a soft but not sticky dough.

5 Sprinkle a little flour over a clean work surface, turn the dough out onto it, and roll out with a rolling pin until it is about ⅛ inch thick. Using the larger cookie cutter, stamp out rounds from the dough.

6 Take the smaller cookie cutter or a small upside-down glass and cut out a small hole in the center of half the large rounds. Remove the center pieces; the cookies with the holes will make the tops. Gather up the leftover trimmings and reroll them to make more circles until all the pastry is used up.

7 Carefully lay the circles on the prepared baking sheets.

8 **Ask an adult to help you** transfer the sheets to the preheated oven and bake the cookies for about 6–8 minutes, until crisp and light golden. Remove the sheets from the oven and let them cool.

9 When the cookies are cold, spread a little jam or chocolate spread over one of the complete rounds and place one of the cookies with the holes on top. Repeat with the remaining cookies, then dust with a little confectioners' sugar. Store in an airtight container until ready to serve.

99

This is a beautiful tart to make for a party; it looks just like the ones you find in lovely Italian pastry shops. A slice of this is like a little bit of summer sunshine on your plate! Glazing the case with chocolate means you can fill the case with the fruit in advance without the pastry getting soggy.

summer fruit tart
crostata di frutta d'estate

2½ oz semisweet chocolate

For the pastry
12 tablespoons butter,
    softened
⅓ cup sugar
1 egg yolk
2 cups all-purpose flour,
    plus extra to sprinkle

For the filling
8 oz mascarpone cheese
2 tablespoons sugar
2¼ lb mixed summer
    berries (such as
    strawberries, raspberries,
    and blueberries)
*a 9-inch loose-bottomed
    tart pan*
a pastry brush

Serves 6

1 To make the pastry, put the butter and sugar into a bowl and beat with a wooden spoon until smooth.

2 Add the egg yolk and beat again until it is well mixed in.

3 Stir in the flour and mix until you get a soft but not sticky dough.

4 Divide the dough in half. Put half into a plastic bag and freeze it to use next time.

5 Sprinkle a little flour over a clean work surface, turn the dough out onto it, and roll out with a rolling pin until it is just a little bit bigger than the tart pan.

6 Sprinkle a little flour over the rolling pin to stop it being sticky. Roll the pastry over the rolling pin, lift it all up, and carefully unroll it over the tart pan.

7 Press the pastry gently into the corners and repair any holes with a little extra pastry.

8 Trim the edges so that the pastry crust is nice and neat, then pop it into the fridge for 30 minutes or so, to firm up.

9 **Ask an adult to help you** preheat the oven to 350°F.

10 Take the tart pan out of the fridge and transfer to the preheated oven. Bake for 10–15 minutes, until crisp and golden. Remove from the oven and let cool.

11 Break the chocolate up into pieces and pop it in a small heatproof bowl. **Ask an adult to help you** set the bowl over a saucepan of gently simmering water, making sure that the bottom of the bowl does not touch the water. Stir the chocolate with a wooden spoon until it has melted. Take it off the heat and let it cool for a while.

12 Using a pastry brush, paint the base of the pastry crust with the melted chocolate and let it set.

13 To make the filling, put the mascarpone and sugar in a bowl and beat until smooth. Spoon it into the tart crust.

14 Scatter the berries evenly over the mascarpone and serve in slices.

The Italians often add almonds to their cakes and it helps to create a wonderfully dense, moist cake. They also like using polenta in cakes—and luckily polenta is now very easy to find in the supermarkets, but fine cornmeal makes a good substitute if necessary. I think this cake is perfect served as a dessert with some fresh fruit but quite a few of the children I know seem to love it with a glass of milk as an afternoon treat and adults seem to enjoy a slice with a cup of coffee too!

almond cake
torta alle mandorle

2 sticks (16 tablespoons)
   butter, softened,
   plus extra to grease
1¼ cups sugar
4 extra-large eggs, cracked
   into a bowl
1⅓ cups ground almonds
⅔ cup polenta
⅓ cup self-rising flour
1 unwaxed lemon
confectioners' sugar,
   to dust
a 9-inch springform
*   cake pan*

Serves 10

1 **Ask an adult to help you** preheat the oven to 300°F.

2 Put a little butter on a paper towel and rub it over the cake pan to grease it. Take the bottom out of the cake pan, lay it on a sheet of parchment paper, and draw around it. Cut out the circle. Put the cake pan back together and lay the paper circle in the bottom of the pan to line it.

3 **Ask an adult to help you** beat the butter and sugar together in a large bowl with an electric whisk until smooth, light, and fluffy.

4 Add the eggs, a little at a time, stirring well between each addition.

5 Stir in the almonds, polenta, and flour.

6 Wash the lemon and **ask an adult to help you** grate the zest (see Tip on page 24). Stir the zest into the bowl and squeeze in the juice from the lemon too.

7 Spoon the mixture evenly into the cake pan. **Ask an adult to help you** transfer the pan to the preheated oven and bake for 45 minutes or so, until the cake has risen and is golden and springy to the touch.

8 **Ask an adult to help you** remove the cake from the oven and let cool for 20 minutes, then turn out onto a wire rack to cool completely. Dust with confectioners' sugar.

These make an indulgent treat for a special breakfast or a cool dessert with ice cream when your friends come around to eat!

fried chocolate sandwiches
sandwich croccanti con cioccolato

**16 small, thin slices
of bread**
3¹/₂ oz mascarpone
**3¹/₂ oz semisweet
chocolate, grated**
5 tablespoons butter

Serves 4

1 Cut the crusts off the bread and spread 8 of the slices with a thin layer of mascarpone.

2 Grate the chocolate with a cheese grater—mind those fingers!—and scatter a nice layer of it over the mascarpone. Put a plain slice of bread on top and press down lightly.

3 **Ask an adult to help you** melt a little butter in a nonstick skillet and fry the sandwiches for about 3 minutes, until the bread is golden and

the chocolate is melting. (You will have to cook the sandwiches in batches, depending on how big your skillet is.)

4 Carefully turn the sandwiches over and fry for a further 2–3 minutes.

5 **Ask an adult to help you** remove the sandwiches from the skillet and cut them in half diagonally. Eat them warm.

This looks every bit as delicious as it tastes. It makes a scrumptious dessert with some ice cream, but is also good for tucking into a lunchbox or picnic hamper.

apple cake
torta di mele

10 tablespoons butter,
   plus extra to grease
3/4 cup sugar
2 eggs, cracked into a bowl
1 cup ground almonds
5 tablespoons all-purpose
   flour
1 teaspoon baking powder
1 unwaxed lemon
6 tablespoons whole milk
2 red apples
confectioners' sugar,
   to dust
a 5 x 9-inch loaf pan

Serves 8–10

1 **Ask an adult to help you** preheat the oven to 300°F.

2 **Ask an adult to help you** melt the butter in a small pan.

3 Put a little butter on a paper towel and rub it over the loaf pan to grease it. Put the pan on a sheet of parchment paper and draw around the base. Cut out the rectangle and lay it in the bottom of the pan to line it.

4 **Ask an adult to help you** beat the butter and sugar together in a large bowl with an electric whisk until smooth, light, and fluffy.

5 Add the eggs, a little at a time, stirring well between each addition.

6 Stir in the almonds, flour, and baking powder.

7 Wash the lemon and **ask an adult to help you** grate the zest (see Tip on page 24). Stir the zest into the bowl along with the milk.

8 Spoon the mixture evenly into the loaf pan.

9 **Ask an adult to help you** cut the apples in half. Remove the cores and cut the flesh into thin slices. Arrange evenly over the cake.

10 **Ask an adult to help you** transfer the pan to the preheated oven and bake for 45 minutes or so, until the cake has risen and is golden and springy to the touch. Remove the cake from the oven and let cool for 20 minutes, then turn out onto a wire rack to cool completely. Dust with confectioners' sugar.

Here's a totally fantastic treat a bit like a rice pudding but richer and only for those who have a really sweet tooth! It's so simple to make because you just have to pop it in the oven where it slowly bakes, getting softer and stickier and lovelier. You have to take it out halfway through cooking to add ingredients, but before you know it, it's ready to eat!

sweet bay-scented risotto

1 cup risotto rice

6 cups milk

½ cup sugar

1 dried bay leaf

a small can of condensed
  milk

3 tablespoons butter,
  plus extra to grease

jam, to serve

an ovenproof dish

Serves 4

1 **Ask an adult to help you** preheat the oven to 300°F.

2 Put a little butter on a paper towel and rub it over the ovenproof dish to grease it.

3 Tip the rice into the dish and stir in 4 cups of the milk and half the sugar.

4 **Ask an adult to help you** transfer the dish to the preheated oven and bake for 30 minutes, until the rice has started to soften.

5 **Ask an adult to help you** remove the dish from the oven and stir in the bay leaf, remaining sugar and milk, and condensed milk. Return to the oven and bake for a further 30 minutes or so, until thickened and creamy.

6 Serve with a spoonful of jam.

This is a lovely sweet in the summer, when juicy, ripe peaches are at their best—but try it with raspberries and strawberries too, or even chopped ripe pears in the winter.

layered peach & mascarpone dessert
coppette alle pesce con mascarpone

4 ripe peaches
½ cup plus 1 tablespoon
   sugar
1 unwaxed lemon
8 oz mascarpone
2 extra-large egg whites
4 sprigs of fresh mint,
   to garnish

Serves 4

1 **Ask an adult to help you** cut the peaches in half and remove the pits, then chop the flesh into small chunks and place them in a bowl. Stir in 1 tablespoon of the sugar.

2 Wash the lemon and **ask an adult to help you** grate the zest (see Tip on page 24). Stir the zest in with the peaches.

3 In a separate bowl, beat the mascarpone and remaining sugar together until smooth.

4 Take another bowl and make sure it is super clean and free of grease. Pour the egg whites into the bowl. **Ask an adult to help you** whisk them with an electric whisk until they are firm enough to stand in soft peaks.

5 Take 2 tablespoons of the egg whites and beat them into the mascarpone to loosen it.

6 Carefully fold the remaining egg whites into the mascarpone mixture using a sort of figure-eight motion.

7 Spoon some of the peaches into the bottom of 4 pretty dessert glasses. Spoon over a layer of the mascarpone mixture.

8 Add another layer of peaches, then another layer of the mascarpone mixture. Top with a couple of pieces of peach and garnish with a sprig of mint.

9 Chill until ready to serve.

These little tarts look so elegant and taste so good, yet are a cinch to make. The way they fly off the plates, you might almost imagine they had wings!

white chocolate & raspberry tartlets
torte con cioccolata bianca e lamponi

10 oz puff pastry dough,
  thawed if frozen
3½ oz white chocolate
2 eggs
6 tablespoons heavy cream
¼ cup sugar
10 oz raspberries
all-purpose flour,
  to sprinkle
confectioners' sugar,
  to dust
a 12-hole muffin pan
a cookie cutter roughly
  the same size as the
  muffin pan holes

Makes 12

1 Ask an adult to help you preheat the oven to 350°F.

2 Sprinkle a little flour over a clean work surface and turn the dough out onto it. Using a rolling pin, roll it out gently until it is about ⅛ inch thick.

3 Cut the dough into rounds using the cookie cutter and press them gently into the muffin pan holes.

4 Break the chocolate up into pieces and pop it in a small heatproof bowl. **Ask an adult to help you** set the bowl over a saucepan of gently simmering water, making sure that the bottom of the bowl does not touch the water. Stir the chocolate with a wooden spoon until it has melted. Take it off the heat and let it cool for a while.

5 Crack the eggs into a large bowl and beat with a wire whisk until smooth.

6 Whisk in the cream and sugar.

7 Whisk in the melted chocolate and make sure the mixture is nice and smooth.

8 Carefully fill the tartlet crusts with the mixture using a small spoon.

9 Ask an adult to help you put the muffin pan in the preheated oven and bake for about 15 minutes, until the pastry is puffy and golden and the filling is risen (don't worry, it will fall as the tartlets cool).

10 Ask an adult to help you remove the pan from the oven and let cool.

11 Put 3 or 4 raspberries on the top of each, dust with confectioners' sugar, and serve.

113

These delicious little chocolate and almond cakes are a specialty of the Abruzzo region of Italy where I have my house. They usually have a pastry lid too but I find them a little bit heavy that way —so this is my version!

abruzzese chocolate & almond tartlets
bocconotti

confectioners' sugar,
  to dust

For the pastry
12 tablespoons butter,
  softened
6 tablespoons sugar
1 egg yolk
2 cups all-purpose flour,
  plus extra to sprinkle

For the filling
3½ oz semisweet chocolate
1 egg white
⅓ cup ground almonds
¼ cup sugar
a 12-hole muffin pan
a cookie cutter roughly
  the same size as the
  muffin pan holes

Makes 12

1 **Ask an adult to help you** preheat the oven to 350°F.

2 To make the pastry, put the butter and sugar into a bowl and beat with a wooden spoon until smooth.

3 Add the egg yolk and beat again until it is well mixed.

4 Stir in the flour and mix until you get a soft but not sticky dough.

5 Divide the dough in half. Put half into a plastic bag and freeze it to use next time.

6 Sprinkle a little flour over a clean work surface, turn the dough out onto it, and roll out with a rolling pin until it is ⅛ inch thick.

7 Cut the dough into rounds using the cookie cutter and press them gently into the muffin pan holes.

8 To make the filling, break the chocolate into little pieces and pop it into a large bowl.

9 Add the egg white, almonds, and sugar and stir until well mixed.

10 Carefully fill the tartlet crusts with the mixture using a small spoon.

11 **Ask an adult to help you** put the muffin pan in the preheated oven and bake for about 5 minutes or so, until the pastry is golden and the chocolate topping looks gooey.

12 **Ask an adult to help you** remove the pan from the oven and let cool.

13 Dust with confectioners' sugar and serve.

114

This is an easy and delicious treat that looks like the savory salamis you see in butcher shops and delicatessens in Italy. It's really easy to make but watch it because adults tend to like this just as much as children do, so you might find it disappears more quickly than you imagined!

chocolate salami
salame di cioccolato

6½ oz milk or semisweet chocolate

3 tablespoons butter

5 oz Petit Beurre cookies, or other plain, buttery cookies

Makes 8–10 slices

1 Break the chocolate up into pieces and pop it in a small heatproof bowl with the butter. **Ask an adult to help you** set the bowl over a saucepan of gently simmering water, making sure that the bottom of the bowl does not touch the water. Stir the mixture with a wooden spoon until it has melted. Take it off the heat and let it cool for a while.

2 Break the cookies into very small pieces (you could pop them into a plastic bag and give them a bash with a rolling pin) but leave some chunky pieces too. Tip them into a bowl.

3 Pour the melted chocolate mixture into the cookie crumbs, making sure to scrape all the chocolate from the side of the bowl. Stir well until evenly mixed.

4 Put your hands right in the bowl and bring the mixture together. Form roughly into a salami shape.

5 Lay a large piece of plastic wrap on the work surface in front of you and pop the chocolate salami onto it.

6 Roll the plastic wrap around it tightly, and as you are doing so, try to pull it into a firm, even salami shape.

7 Twirl the ends of the plastic wrap together, then pop it into the fridge to set for an hour or so.

8 Serve in slices.

117

Imagine your favorite storebought strawberry ice cream. It's utterly yummy, isn't it? Well now you can make your own and I guarantee it will be a hundred times better than any you've tried before. Serve it by itself in a bowl for dessert, or pop a scoop onto a waffle cone and enjoy on a summer's afternoon.

strawberry ice cream
gelato di fragole

2 lb strawberries
3/4 cup sugar
8 oz mascarpone
*an ice-cream maker
(optional)*

Serves about 6

1 Pull the hulls off the strawberries and throw them away. **Ask an adult to help you** pop the strawberries in a blender and whiz them until smooth.

2 Add the sugar and mascarpone and **ask an adult to help you** whiz the mixture until everything is well mixed.

3 Transfer to an ice-cream maker and freeze according to the manufacturer's instructions.

4 If you don't have an ice-cream maker, pour the mixture into a freezerproof container and pop it in the freezer until almost frozen.

5 Remove the container from the freezer and beat well with a whisk to remove any ice crystals. Return the container to the freezer.

6 Repeat once more, then freeze until solid.

7 Transfer to the fridge about 20 minutes before serving.

Deliciously creamy plain ice cream with crunchy bits
of semisweet chocolate—an irresistible after-school treat!

ice cream with chocolate shards
stracciatella

1 **Ask an adult to help you** put the milk, mascarpone, and sugar in a blender and whiz until smooth.

2 Transfer to an ice-cream maker and freeze according to the manufacturer's instructions.

3 Meanwhile, break the chocolate up into pieces and pop it in a small heatproof bowl. **Ask an adult to help you** set the bowl over a saucepan of gently simmering water, making sure that the bottom of the bowl does not touch the water. Stir the chocolate with a wooden spoon until it has melted. Take it off the heat and let it cool for a while.

4 When the ice cream is almost frozen, drizzle in the chocolate, little by little. Stir between drizzles. The chocolate will solidify as soon as it touches the ice cream.

5 If you don't have an ice-cream maker, pour the mixture into a freezerproof container and pop it in the freezer until almost frozen.

6 Remove the container from the freezer and beat well with a whisk to remove any ice crystals. Return the container to the freezer.

7 **Ask an adult to help you** chop the chocolate into tiny pieces, then remove the container from the freezer, beat well, and stir in the chocolate pieces. Freeze again until solid.

8 Transfer to the fridge about 20 minutes before serving.

1 cup milk
8 oz mascarpone
$\frac{1}{2}$ cup sugar
$3\frac{1}{2}$ oz semisweet chocolate
*an ice-cream maker
(optional)*
Serves about 6

Sometimes it's best to keep things simple. This is a milky ice cream that is so satisfying it needs no other flavoring.

creamy milk ice cream
fioridilatte

1 **Ask an adult to help you** put the milk, mascarpone, and sugar in a blender and whiz until smooth.

2 Transfer to an ice-cream maker and freeze according to the manufacturer's instructions.

3 If you don't have an ice-cream maker, pour the mixture into a freezerproof container and pop it in the freezer until almost frozen.

4 Remove the container from the freezer and beat well with a whisk to remove any ice crystals. Return the container to the freezer.

5 Repeat once more, then freeze until solid.

6 Transfer to the fridge about 20 minutes before serving.

$1^3/_4$ cups milk
8 oz mascarpone
$\frac{1}{2}$ cup sugar
*an ice-cream maker
(optional)*
Serves about 6

120

Affogato is a classic Italian dessert which is simply vanilla ice cream with a hot, super-strong espresso coffee poured over it just before serving so that all the coffee trickles down and starts to melt the ice cream. Strong coffee is something that grows on you as you get older, so here's a totally irresistible variation using hot raspberry sauce.

Try to find an ice-cube tray with larger-than-normal cubes in fancy shapes if you can for these tasty treats. Otherwise, simply use Dixie cups.

little iced fruit spoons
gelati cucchiaio

Strawberry
1 cup strawberries
2 tablespoons sugar
a squeeze of lemon juice
(optional)

Raspberry
1 cup raspberries
2 tablespoons sugar
a squeeze of lemon juice
(optional)
an ice-cube tray or
6 Dixie cups
tiny plastic or metal spoons

Makes about 6

Peach
2 ripe peaches, pitted
2 tablespoons sugar
a squeeze of lemon juice
(optional)

Mango
1 ripe mango, peeled and
pitted
2 tablespoons sugar
a squeeze of lemon juice
(optional)

1 Ask an adult to help you put the fruit, sugar, 2 tablespoons water, and a squeeze of lemon juice in a blender and whiz until smooth.

2 Pour the mixture into the ice-cube tray or Dixie cups, pop a little spoon in each, and freeze for a couple of hours.

raspberry affogato

1 lb fresh or frozen
raspberries
4–5 tablespoons sugar
vanilla ice cream, to serve
a nylon strainer

Serves 4

1 Put just over half the raspberries in the strainer and push them with the back of a spoon through the strainer into a saucepan.

2 Stir the sugar into the raspberry juice in the pan and **ask an adult to help you** heat it gently until the sugar dissolves.

3 Stir in the remaining raspberries.

4 Place scoops of ice cream into dessert bowls. Pour the hot raspberry sauce over the top and serve immediately.

These little sandwiches made from light wafer-like cookies and mini-scoops of luscious lemony iced yogurt are to die for. Serve with a glass of ice-cold milk.

little lemon iced yogurt sandwiches
mini sandwich al gelato di yogurt limone

2 oz semisweet chocolate

For the iced yogurt
1 large, juicy unwaxed
    lemon
2 cups plain yogurt
    (not reduced-fat)
½ cup sugar

For the wafers
3 tablespoons butter,
    softened
¼ cup sugar
2 egg whites
5 tablespoons all-purpose
    flour
an ice-cream maker
    (optional)
2 baking sheets, lined with
    parchment paper

Makes about 6

1 To make the iced yogurt, wash the lemon and **ask an adult to help you** grate the zest (see Tip on page 24). Stir the zest into a large bowl and squeeze in the juice from the lemon.

2 Add the yogurt and sugar and beat everything until smooth.

3 Transfer to an ice-cream maker and freeze according to the manufacturer's instructions.

4 If you don't have an ice-cream maker, pour the mixture into a freezerproof container and pop it in the freezer until almost frozen.

5 Remove the container from the freezer and beat well with a whisk to remove any ice crystals. Return the container to the freezer.

6 Repeat once more, then freeze until solid.

7 Transfer to the fridge about 20 minutes before serving.

8 Meanwhile, make the wafers. **Ask an adult to help you** preheat the oven to 350°F.

9 Put the butter and sugar into a bowl and beat with a wooden spoon until smooth.

10 Add the egg whites and beat again until well mixed.

11 Add in the flour and beat until smooth.

12 Place little spoonfuls of the mixture onto the baking sheets and swirl around with the back of a spoon to make thin rounds with a diameter of about 1–1½ inches.

13 **Ask an adult to help you** put the sheets in the preheated oven and bake for about 8–10 minutes, until golden.

14 **Ask an adult to help you** remove them from the oven and let cool.

15 Meanwhile, break the chocolate up into pieces and pop it in a small heatproof bowl. **Ask an adult to help you** set the bowl over a saucepan of gently simmering water, making sure that the bottom of the bowl does not touch the water. Stir the chocolate with a wooden spoon until it has melted. Take it off the heat and let it cool for a while.

16 Dip a fork into the melted chocolate and pass it to and fro over the wafers to make a pretty pattern. Let set.

17 When you are ready to make up the mini-sandwiches, simply sandwich 2 wafers together with a scoop of the iced yogurt and eat at once!

index

conversion chart

Weights and measures have been rounded up or down slightly to make measuring easier.

Measuring butter:
A US stick of butter weighs 4 oz which is approximately 115 g or 8 tablespoons.

The recipes in this book require the following conversions:

American	Metric	Imperial
6 tbsp	85 g	3 oz
7 tbsp	100 g	3 1/2 oz
1 stick	115 g	4 oz

Volume equivalents:

American	Metric	Imperial
1 teaspoon	5 ml	
1 tablespoon	15 ml	
1/4 cup	60 ml	2 fl oz
1/3 cup	75 ml	2 1/2 fl oz
1/2 cup	125 ml	4 fl oz
2/3 cup	150 ml	5 fl oz (1/4 pint)
3/4 cup	175 ml	6 fl oz
1 cup	250 ml	8 fl oz

Weight equivalents:

Imperial	Metric
1 oz	30 g
2 oz	55 g
3 oz	85 g
3 1/2 oz	100 g
4 oz	115 g
6 oz	175 g
8 oz (1/2 lb)	225 g
9 oz	250 g
10 oz	280 g
12 oz	350 g
13 oz	375 g
14 oz	400 g
15 oz	425 g
16 oz (1 lb)	450 g

Measurements:

Inches	cm
1/4 inch	5 mm
1/2 inch	1 cm
1 inch	2.5 cm
2 inches	5 cm
3 inches	7 cm
4 inches	10 cm
5 inches	12 cm
6 inches	15 cm
7 inches	18 cm
8 inches	20 cm
9 inches	23 cm
10 inches	25 cm
11 inches	28 cm
12 inches	30 cm

Oven temperatures:

120°C	(250°F)	Gas 1/2
140°C	(275°F)	Gas 1
150°C	(300°F)	Gas 2
170°C	(325°F)	Gas 3
180°C	(350°F)	Gas 4
190°C	(375°F)	Gas 5
200°C	(400°F)	Gas 6
220°C	(425°F)	Gas 7

author's acknowledgments

With massive thanks to the fantastic team at Ryland Peters & Small for helping to produce a very beautiful book of which I am hugely proud; to Lisa for the stunning photography, and to Joy and Liz for the fabulous styling and props. A big, big thank you to each of the gorgeous children, whose sunny smiles have helped light up the pages and bring the book to life. *Grazie mille* to Italy for the fabulous food and special friends I have discovered through living here. And lastly but by no means least, oodles of thanks and oceans of love to my own family—my wonderful, supportive parents for teaching me to delight in good food throughout my own childhood, and my three treasured sons, Chris, Oli, and Tim for being such a constant joy to cook for.

publisher's acknowledgments

The publisher would like to thank the wonderful models Alexandra and Darcy; Billy and Cormac; DJ; Evelyn and Elodie; Georgia; Havana; Isabella and Jamie; Jessica; Linus; Ruby and Lola; Marly; Rhianna; and Ruby, Savannah, and Jack.